Typesetting with LaTeX: a guide for novices

by

N. Edward Matavka

Set in Antykwa Torunska, 12 point.
ISBN 978-0-9917682-1-9

CHECKSHEET
for the LaTeX Author/Editor Hat Course

"HAT": On a train, a locomotive engineer and a conductor each wear a different kind of hat. You will notice that various jobs in society are designated by different hats. From this we get the word "hat" as a slang term meaning one's specialised duties.

NAME: _________________________________
SCHOOL: ______________________________
DATE STARTED: _______________
COMPLETED: _______________

LENGTH OF COURSE: This course is expected to take six months, if studied at the rate of ninety minutes per day.

IDEAL SCENE: Ideally, the end product of this course will be a student who can make effective use of the LaTeX document preparation system for typesetting books, reports, and technical articles in scientific and mathematical journals.

REALITY FACTOR: You are expected to apply your LaTeX knowledge to your immediate studies. You are expected to demonstrate your ability to apply the course materials by using what you have learned in your other assignments and projects.

Section N: Orientation

1. READ "What is LaTeX?" ____
2. DEMO. A markup language. ____
3. ESSAY. In your own words, compare and contrast LaTeX and Microsoft Word. When might LaTeX be superior?____
4. READ "Author, Designer, and Typesetter" ____
5. READ "What is Plain Text?" ____
6. READ "A Typical LaTeX Input File" ____
7. READ "Characters and Control Sequences" ____
8. GRAPHIC DEMO. The anatomy of a LaTeX document. ____

Section I: Basic LaTeX Usage

1. READ "Producing a LaTeX Input File" ____
2. READ "The document Environment" ____
3. READ "Producing Text Documents with LaTeX" ____
4. PRACTICAL. Typeset a text of your preference using LaTeX. Save this document. ____
5. READ "Blank Spaces and Carriage Returns in the Input File" ____
6. READ "Quotation Marks and Dashes" ____
7. PRACTICAL. Add a fictional dialogue of your preference to the filc you created earlier. ____
8. READ “Changing Fonts in Text Mode” ____

9. PRACTICAL. Italicise the following sentence properly and add it to your portfolio:
   "Please don't do that," Charlie said fretfully. ____
10. PRACTICAL. Italicise the following sentence properly and add it to your portfolio:
   Tensor Calculus, by John Synge and Alfred Schild ____
11. PRACTICAL. Copy out a paragraph from a book of your choice, and make the text \Large size using an environment. Save it to your portfolio document. ____
12. READ "Accents Used in Text". ____
13. PRACTICAL. Typeset the following French text in Latex:

   "Portez ce vieux whisky au juge blond qui fume sur son île intérieure, à côté de l'alcôve ovoïde, où les bûches se consument dans l'âtre, ce qui lui permet de penser à la cænogénèse de l'être dont il est question dans la cause ambiguë entendue à Moÿ, dans un capharnaüm qui, pense-t-il, diminue çà et là la qualité de son œuvre." ____
14. READ "Active Characters and Special Symbols in Text". ____
15. READ "Footnotes and Marginal Notes". ____

16. ESSAY. When would a footnote be optimal? When would a marginal note be optimal? ____
17. READ "Commenting". ____
18. PRACTICAL. Place a comment above each of the sections of your portfolio, describing what you did. ____

<u>Section II: LaTeX Structures</u>

1. READ "The Structure of Text and Language." ____
2. PRACTICAL. Transcribe a newspaper or magazine article of your choice. Use French spacing. Place a comment above it. ____
3. READ "Logical Headings in LaTeX". ____
4. PRACTICAL. Section your portfolio document by replacing your comments with logical headings. ____
5. READ "Line Breaking and Page Breaking". ____
6. READ “Tags, Declarations, and Environments”. ____
7. GRAPHIC DEMO. The form of a LaTeX document, with environments properly placed. ____
8. READ "Title and Author". ____
9. PRACTICAL. Title your portfolio document "My Portfolio" and sign your name. ____
10. READ “Abstracts". ____

11. PRACTICAL. Create an abstract for your portfolio. Title it "Executive Summary". ____
12. READ "Alignment". ____
13. PRACTICAL. Transcribe a paragraph from a non-fiction book of your choice. Duplicate it thrice, and align it to the left, centre, and right, respectively. ____
14. READ “Lists”. ____
15. PRACTICAL. Create an itemised, enumerated, and description list. Insert the appropriate headings. ____
16. Read “Displayed Quotations”. ____
17. PRACTICAL. Find a quote that inspires you. Quote it properly in LaTeX, under the appropriate heading. Give credit to the source. ____
18. READ “Verse”. ____
19. PRACTICAL. Find a verse quote from a play by William Shakespeare. Quote it properly and give credit to the play. ____
20. READ “Prepared Text”. ____
21. ESSAY. Under which circumstances might the prepared text function best be used? ____
22. PRACTICAL. Use the prepared text function to typeset a program source code listing. ____
23. READ “Tables”. ____
24. PRACTICAL. Create a table. ____
25. READ “Document Classes”. ____

26. READ "Producing Letters". ____
27. PRACTICAL. Write a business letter in LaTeX syntax. Save it separately from your portfolio. ____
28. READ "Slides". ____

Section III: Advanced Features

1. READ "User-Defined Control Sequences in LaTeX." ____
2. READ "The pagestyle command". ____
3. READ "Extra Line Spacing". ____
4. PRACTICAL. Make your portfolio one-and-a-half spaced. ____
5. READ "In-Paragraph Lists". ____
6. PRACTICAL. Construct an in-paragraph list at the end of your portfolio. Add an appropriate heading. ____
7. READ "Chemistry". ____
8. PRACTICAL. Transcribe an appropriate chemical article or part of a chemistry book into LaTeX. Ensure that it contains at least one chemical equation. Add the appropriate heading. ____
9. READ "Line-Wrapped Tables". ____
10. PRACTICAL. Find an actuarial table for life insurance. Transcribe the last ten years into LaTeX. ____
11. READ "Colours". ____
12. PRACTICAL. Find an entry that interests you in an encyclopaedia of your choice. Transcribe it into

LaTeX, making sure that every headword is coloured magenta. ____

Section IV: Mathematics

This checksheet could easily have included the various sections on typesetting mathematical text in LaTeX. It doesn't, for one simple reason: the 'language' of mathematical signs and symbols is, at the same time, too broad and too abstruse to teach every student as a matter of course. Therefore, devising an appropriate mathematical checksheet for the student's present or future leanings is left as an exercise for the teacher/supervisor, or, if the course is self-supervised, for the student himself.

Contents

Preface

Several years ago, I was compelled to learn the intricacies of the LaTeX typesetting engine owing to academic reasons. There was no official course to teach me, which was something I had no problem with, as I learn well in an autodidactic environment. I quickly learned two facts about LaTeX: first, that it was essentially analogous to a rudimentary version of HTML, and second, that its capabilities in the area of mathematical typesetting were beyond comparison.

Unfortunately, in addition to being the number one benefit of using LaTeX, the easy-to-use equation syntax is also its worst flaw. The immediate forerunner of LaTeX was written by a disgruntled mathematics professor who, in the late 1970's, had become irritated with the various *faux pas* committed by the layout designers who worked at his publisher's. He had especially become frustrated at their inability, in his view, to use space effectively.

The professor claimed that he could get a computer to mock up a better page layout than did the professional layout designers, and that he could get it to do so within the space of a year. Although the second part of his boast turned out to be patently wrong (his layout engine took nearly ten years to mature before his book was published in it), he had discovered a new branch of computer science on his way there.

LaTeX itself was also written by a professor, although he was one of computer science rather than mathematics; he had grown tired of TeX's mind-twisting complexity and needed something that would do the heavy lifting automatically. It is my belief that he succeeded in this regard.

Unfortunately, what nobody succeeded in was bringing LaTeX to the world. Product literature makes a point of describing its mathematical capabilities; so do the unofficial tutorials, handbooks, and guides. In fact, the great majority of LaTeX guidebooks available are geared chiefly towards undergraduate students of the Mathematics tripos, and other allied fields. Physics, for one, is given almost as much emphasis, but other Natural Sciences students have no such luck, despite LaTeX being just as good in typesetting chemical and biological text. Even students of the humanities, as well as the law, would benefit from learning how properly to use LaTeX; it is miles ahead of any word processor on the planet in most respects.

My aim in writing this guide was to redress this imbalance. That is not to say that this book is not about mathematical typesetting; of course it is. Maths are an integral feature of LaTeX and one to be celebrated rather than reviled;

however, in writing this guide, I have taken the conscious decision not to place maths at the front and centre. In fact, one could learn all the basic and advanced LaTeX features covered in this guide without learning how to enter a single mathematical symbol.

For example, rather than use purely didactic examples (*i.e.*, "Hello, world!", "This is a title", etc.), or examples taken purely from mathematical books, I have made the deliberate choice to rely on extracts from textbooks on a wide array of subjects, from classic English literature to chemistry. This stylistic decision should keep you challenged, but not challenged enough to give in; it should also fit a wide range of skill levels, but not such that a moderately-skilled user would find it patronising.

I hope you enjoy running this course as much as I enjoyed writing it.

Chapter 1

Introduction to LaTeX

1.1 What is LaTeX?

LaTeX is a computer programme for typesetting documents. It takes a computer file, prepared according to certain syntactic rules, and converts it to a form that may be printed on a high-quality printer, such as a laser writer, to produce a printed document of a quality comparable with good quality books and journals. Simple documents that do not contain mathematical formulæ or tables may be produced very easily: effectively all one has to do is to type the text straight in (observing certain rules relating to quotation marks and punctuation dashes). Typesetting mathematics is somewhat more complex, but even here LaTeX is comparatively straightforward to use when one considers the complexity of some of the formulæ, and the number of mathematical symbols, which it has to produce.

LaTeX is what is known as a *markup language*. A markup language is a way of *annotating*, or 'marking up', a document in a way that is *syntactically distinguishable* from the text—*i.e.*, that a human reader can tell the text and the annotations apart. Markup languages evolved from the editors' practice of marking up, or "blue-pencilling", an author's manuscript using certain internationally-recognised symbols, or *obelisms*—traditionally with a non-xeroxable blue pencil. Since computers do not understand scribbles in blue pencil, a different notation was derived: certain symbols would separate the instructions for the computer (*i.e.*, the markup) from the document text.

The language in which Web pages on the Internet are written is a markup language. If a Web page is opened in a *text editor*, such as vim, you will see certain commands telling the Web browser to make text bold or italic, to insert a heading, to construct a table, or to change colours. It follows from this that a Web page can be written with nothing but a text editor. HTML, troff, RTF, PostScript, and LaTeX are all markup languages; documents can be written in each using a text editor. HTML is used for Web pages, PostScript for controlling printers, and troff, RTF, and LaTeX for writing articles and books.

A markup language stands in contrast to *word processing*. A word-processed document is both created and edited using a special programme; the user enters commands into the programme, and it applies those changes to the document. In word processing, formatting usually involves telling the computer, for example, to make the text `CHAPTER ONE` bold and 24-point size; in a markup language, the user simply commands the computer to make the text a heading, and the computer does the rest. The table of contents, too, is done manually in a word processing programme.

LaTeX is one of a number of 'dialects' of the TeX markup language, all based on the original, 'Plain' version of TeX created by D. E. Knuth. LaTeX, created by L. B. Lamport, is particularly suited to the production of long articles and books, since it has facilities for the automatic numbering of chapters, sections, theorems, equations etc., and also has facilities for cross-referencing. It is probably one of the most suitable versions of TeX for beginners to use.

1.2 Author, Designer, and Typesetter

To publish something, authors give their typed manuscript to a publishing company. One of their book designers then decides the layout of the document (column width, fonts, space before and after headings, ...). The book designer writes his instructions into the manuscript and then gives it to a typesetter, who typesets the book according to these instructions.

A human book designer tries to find out what the author had in mind while writing the manuscript. He decides on chapter headings, citations, examples, formulæ, etc. based on his professional knowledge and from the contents of the manuscript. He does not decide on minutiæ, such as the spacing between individual letters in a word; that is left to the typesetter, who is a professional in that field.

In a way, LaTeX is substantially the same; it is, in essence, an electronic analogue of a book designer, while TeX assumes the mantle of a typesetter. Just like a designer, LaTeX attempts to divine the author's desired layout, based not only on the contents of the manuscript, but also on its own professional knowledge (that is, its programming). Like its human brethren, though, it does not interfere with the fine details, unless the author specifically requests a change; it leaves the job of fine adjustment to TeX the typesetter. The only difference between a flesh-and-blood book designer and the electronic version provided by LaTeX is that the latter does not understand English; it uses its own language, which the author must learn in order to communicate with it.

This is quite different from the WYSIWYG[1] approach that most modern word processors, such as Microsoft Word or LibreOffice, take. With these applications, authors specify the document layout interactively while typing text into the computer. They can see on the screen how the final work will look when it is printed.

When engaging the services of a designer, an author does not typically receive an updated design after every minor change made—the cost, not to mention the inconvenience, would be prohibitive. Instead, he receives a succession of so-called 'galley proofs' only when the hard work of actually composing the text is finished. This, broadly speaking, is the best method for operating LaTeX as well. It is most prudent to run LaTeX periodically, but not so often as to be distracting from the main goal—writing.

[1]What you see is what you get.

1.3 What is Plain Text?

LaTeX is a markup language which takes plain text as input and produces a device independent, formatted file as output. For this sentence to be meaningful, each of these terms must also be meaningful. The meaning of most of the other terms was established above, but the phrase *plain text* is a particularly important one.

For the purposes of standard LaTeX, plain text consists of only those characters that are available on a standard American keyboard. More technically, standard LaTeX supports the lower 128 bits of the American Standard Code for Information Interchange (ASCII).

It follows logically from this that LaTeX can create mathematical symbols, accented letters, and all the other things one might expect from a professionally-typeset article or book from nothing more than the characters on one's keyboard.

There are modernised versions of TeX and LaTeX, known as XeTeX and XeLaTeX, which provide support for TrueType fonts as well as a standard called Unicode. When using XeTeX and XeLaTeX, one can enter accented characters, as well as foreign alphabets, into the source file directly; this effectively renders the classic LaTeX commands for accented characters otiose.

This guide, however, works equally well for plain LaTeX and XeLaTeX. It includes no more than what plain LaTeX is compatible with.

1.4 A Typical LaTeX Input File

In order to produce a document using LaTeX, a suitable *input file* must first be created on the computer. The LaTeX program is then applied to the input file and then the printer is used to print out the so-called 'DVI' file produced by the LaTeX program (after first using another program to translate the 'DVI' file into a form that the printer can understand). Here is an example of a typical LaTeX input file:

```
\documentclass[a4paper,12pt]{article}
\begin{document}
The foundations of the rigorous study of
\textit{analysis} were laid in the nineteenth
century, notably by the mathematicians Cauchy
and Weierstrass.  Central to the study of this
subject are the formal definitions of
\textit{limits} and \textit{continuity}.
```

```
Let \(D\) be a subset of \(\bfshape R\) and let
\(f \colon D \to \textbf{R}\) be a real-valued
function on \(D\). The function \(f\) is said
to be \textit{continuous} on \(D\) if, for all
\(\epsilon > 0\) and for all \(x \in D\), there
exists some \(\delta > 0\) (which may depend on
\(x\)) such that if \(y \in D\) satisfies

\[ |y - x| < \delta \]

then

\[ |f(y) - f(x)| < \epsilon. \]

One may readily verify that if \(f\) and \(g\)
are continuous functions on \(D\) then the
functions \(f+g\), \(f-g\) and \(f.g\) are
continuous. If in addition \(g\) is everywhere
non-zero then \(f/g\) is continuous.

\end{document}
```

Applying LaTeX to these paragraphs produces the text

> The foundations of the rigorous study of *analysis* were laid in the nineteenth century, notably by the mathematicians Cauchy and Weierstrass. Central to the study of this subject are the formal definitions of *limits* and *continuity*.
>
> Let D be a subset of $\mathbf{R}$ and let $f\colon D \to \mathbf{R}$ be a real-valued function on D. The function f is said to be *continuous* on D if, for all $\epsilon > 0$ and for all $x \in D$, there exists some $\delta > 0$ (which may depend on x) such that if $y \in D$ satisfies
>
> $$|y - x| < \delta$$
>
> then
>
> $$|f(y) - f(x)| < \epsilon.$$
>
> One may readily verify that if f and g are continuous functions on D then the functions $f + g$, $f - g$ and $f.g$ are continuous. If in addition g is everywhere non-zero then f/g is continuous.

This example illustrates various features of LaTeX. The lines

```
\documentclass[a4paper,12pt]{article}
\begin{document}
```

are placed at the beginning of the input file, followed by the main body of the text and the concluding line

```
\end{document}
```

Although most characters occurring in this file have their usual meaning, there are special characters such as \, $, { and } that have meanings peculiar to LaTeX. In particular, there are sequences of characters which begin with a 'backslash' \ which are used to produce mathematical symbols and Greek letters and to accomplish tasks such as changing fonts. These sequences of characters are known as *control sequences*.

1.5 Characters & Control Sequences

Most characters on the keyboard, such as letters and numbers, have their usual meaning. The characters

```
\ { } \( ^ _ % ~ # &
```

are, however, used for special purposes within LaTeX. Therefore, typing one of these characters will not produce the corresponding character in the final document. These characters are very rarely used in ordinary text, though, and there are methods of producing them when they are required in the final document.

In order to typeset a mathematical document, it is necessary to produce a considerable number of special mathematical symbols. One also needs to be able to change fonts. Also mathematical documents often contain arrays of numbers or symbols (matrices) and other complex expressions. These are produced in LaTeX using *control sequences.* Most control sequences consist of a backslash \ followed by a string of (upper or lower case) letters. For example, `\alpha`, `\textit` and `\sum` are control sequences.

In the example above, the control sequences `\textit` and `\textbf` were used to change the font to *italic* and **boldface** respectively, and the control sequences `\to`, `\in`, `\delta` and `\epsilon` were used to produce the mathematical symbols $\to$ and $\in$ and the Greek letters δ and ϵ

There is another variety of control sequence which consists of a backslash followed by a *single* character that is not a letter. Examples of control sequences of this sort are `\{`, `\"` and `\$`.

Another example of a single-character control sequence is \(and its partner, \). The first is used when one is changing from ordinary text to a mathematical expression, and the second is used when changing back to ordinary text. In Plain TeX, the dollar sign is used in both circumstances; this is still permitted in LaTeX to preserve backwards compatibility, but it is considered old-fashioned. \[and \] are also used to input mathematical expressions; the difference in usage is that \(and \) are used when the equation is inside of a paragraph, and \[and \] are used when the equation is to be set in its own line.

The special characters { and } are used for *grouping* purposes. Everything enclosed within a matching pair of such brackets is treated as a single unit. These brackets in the example above can be seen to group characters set in a font different from the default; other instances will be seen where { and } are used in LaTeX to group words and symbols together (e.g., when producing superscripts and subscripts which contain more than one symbol).

The remaining special characters

```
^ _ % ~ # &
```

have special purposes within LaTeX that shall be established later in this book.

Chapter 2

Producing Simple Documents using LaTeX

2.1 Producing a LaTeX Input File

The first line of a LaTeX input file must consist of a `\documentclass` control sequence. The recommended such control sequence for articles in scientific and technical journals, and similar documents, has the form

```
\documentclass[12pt]{article}
```

Please do not worry about what this control sequence means when first learning to use LaTeX: its meaning will be fully explained in due time, but, in general, its effect is to ensure that the text is of a size that is easy to read. There are variants of this `\documentclass` control sequence which are appropriate for letters or for books.

The `documentclass` control sequence may be followed by certain other optional control sequences, such as the `\pagestyle` control sequence. It is not necessary to find out about most of these control sequences when first learning to use LaTeX. After all of these comes the control sequence which officially starts the main part of the document:

```
\begin{document}
```

This control sequence is then followed by the main body of the text, in the format prescribed by the rules of LaTeX.

Finally, the input file ends with a line containing the control sequence

```
\end{document}
```

2.2 The document Environment

LaTeX is a highly structured format for writing articles, books, reports, and letters. Instead of focussing on cosmetic details such as fonts, margins, and indents, LaTeX focusses on the structural hierarchy of the document.

It does this by what are known as environments. An environment is a form of *group* that identifies a particular section of text as being, for example, a bulleted list, and prescribes a particular course of special treatment. Of all these, the most basic and rudimentary is the `document` environment: it identifies text as being in the document.

The `document` environment is bounded by the control sequences `\begin{document}` and `\end{document}`; this is the case for all environments.

Everything within the `document` environment affects printed output: the content itself, the font styles, the table of contents, and the document hierarchy all go into this environment.

Any extensions to the way LaTeX usually functions go before this environment; this section is called the *preamble* or the *header*. Similarly, a document's *metadata* (the data about its data), such as the name of its author, its title, the date it was written on, and other such things, go before the

\begin{document}. Nothing goes after this environment.

In learning about LaTeX, you will learn about many more environments. Each has the same purpose as was described here: an environment encapsulates text that gets some sort of special treatment. In this particular case, the special treatment the text gets is being printed. The syntax for an environment is always the same: it is opened by \begin{blah} and closed by \end{blah}.

2.3 Producing Text Documents with LaTeX

To produce a simple document using LaTeX, one should create a LaTeX input file, beginning with a \documentclass control sequence and the \begin{document} control sequence, as previously described. The input file should end with the \end{document} control sequence, and the text of the document should be sandwiched between the \begin{document} and \end{document} control sequences, as detailed in this section.

If the document is merely to contain ordinary text, rather than complex mathematical formulæ or special effects such as font changes, then it simply needs to be entered into the computer as is, leaving a completely blank line between successive paragraphs. Do not worry about paragraph indentation: unless special action is taken to over-ride its conventions, LaTeX will automatically indent all paragraphs with the exception of the first paragraph of a new section.

For example, if a document needs only to contain the following text:

> If one merely wishes to type in ordinary text, without complex mathematical formulæ or special effects such as font changes, then one merely has to type it in as it is, leaving a completely blank line between successive paragraphs.
>
> You do not have to worry about paragraph indentation: all paragraphs will be indented with the exception of the first paragraph of a new section. One must take care to distinguish between the 'left quote' and the 'right quote' on the computer terminal. Also, one should use two 'single quote' characters in succession if one requires "double quotes". One should never use the (undirected) 'double quote' character on the computer terminal, since the computer is unable

> to tell whether it is a 'left quote' or a 'right quote'. One also has to take care with dashes: a single dash is used for hyphenation, whereas three dashes in succession are required to produce a dash of the sort used for punctuation—such as the one used in this sentence.

it can be produced with an input file containing only:

```
\documentclass[a4paper,12pt]{article}
\begin{document}

If one merely wishes to type in ordinary text,
without complex mathematical formul\ae\ or
special effects such as font changes, then one
merely has to type it in as it is, leaving a
completely blank line between successive
paragraphs.

You do not have to worry about paragraph
indentation: all paragraphs will be indented
with the exception of the first paragraph of a
new section.
```

```
One must take care to distinguish between the
`left quote' and the `right quote' on the
computer terminal.  Also, one should use two
`single quote' characters in succession if one
requires ``double quotes''.  One should never
use the (undirected) `double quote' character
on the computer terminal, since the computer is
unable to tell whether it is a `left quote' or
a `right quote'.  One also has to take care
with dashes: a single dash is used for
hyphenation, whereas three dashes in succession
are required to produce a dash of the sort used
for punctuation---such as the one used in this
sentence.

\end{document}
```

The input file having been created, it must then be run through the LaTeX program and the resulting output file (known as a 'DVI', or *device independent* file) then converted into a form the printer can understand (Portable Document File or PostScript file).

2.4 Blank Spaces & Carriage Returns in the Input File

LaTeX treats the carriage return at the end of a line as though it were a blank space. Similarly, LaTeX treats tab characters as blank spaces. Moreover, LaTeX regards a sequence of blank spaces as though it were a single space, and similarly it will ignore blank spaces at the beginning or end of a line in the input file. Thus, for example, the input

```
This is
    a
        silly
  example   of   a
file with many spaces.



                   This is the beginning
of a new paragraph.
```

produces

This is a silly example of a file with many spaces.

This is the beginning of a new paragraph.

It follows immediately from this that the same results occur whether one types one space or two spaces after a full stop: LaTeX does not distinguish between the two cases.

Any spaces which follow a control sequence will be ignored.

If a blank space in the final document is required following whatever is produced by the control sequence, it must be preceded by a *backslash* \. Thus the sentence

> LaTeX is a very powerful computer typesetting program.

is produced by typing

```
\LaTeX\ is a very powerful computer typesetting
program.
```

The control sequence `\LaTeX` is here used to produce the LaTeX logo.

In general, preceding a blank space by a backslash forces LaTeX to include the blank space in the final document.

2.5 Quotation Marks and Dashes

Single quotation marks are produced in LaTeX using ` and '. Double quotation marks are produced by typing `` and ''. The undirected double quote character " produces double right quotation marks: it should *never* be used where left quotation marks are required.

LaTeX allows you to produce dashes of various length, known as 'hyphens', 'en-dashes' and 'em-dashes'. Hyphens are obtained in LaTeX by typing -, en-dashes by typing -- and em-dashes by typing ---.

En-dashes (so named because they are the width of the lowercase letter 'n') are used when specifying a range of numbers, for example:

```
on pages 155--219.
```

Dashes used for punctuating are often typeset as em-dashes, especially in older books. These are obtained by typing ---.

The dialogue

> "You *were* a little grave," said Alice.
>
> "Well just then I was inventing a new way of getting over a gate—would you like to hear it?"

> "Very much indeed," Alice said politely.
>
> "I'll tell you how I came to think of it," said the Knight. "You see, I said to myself 'The only difficulty is with the feet: the *head* is high enough already.' Now, first I put my head on the top of the gate—then the head's high enough—then I stand on my head—then the feet are high enough, you see—then I'm over, you see."[1]

illustrates the use of quotation marks and dashes. It is obtained in LaTeX from the following input:

```
``You \emph{were} a little grave,'' said
Alice.

``Well just then I was inventing a new way of
getting over a gate---would you like to hear
it?''

``Very much indeed,'' Alice said politely.

``I'll tell you how I came to think of it,''
said the Knight.  ``You see, I said to myself
```

[1] from *Alice through the Looking Glass*, by Lewis Carroll

```
‘The only difficulty is with the feet: the
\emph{head} is high enough already.’ Now,
first I put my head on the top of the
gate---then the head’s high enough---then I
stand on my head---then the feet are high
enough, you see---then I’m over, you
see.’’\footnote{from {\it Alice through the
Looking Glass}, by Lewis Carroll}
```

Sometimes single quotes are required immediately following double quotes, or vice versa, as in

> “I regard computer typesetting as being reasonably ‘straightforward’ ” he said.

The way to typeset this correctly in LaTeX is to use the control sequence `\,` between the quotation marks, so as to obtain the necessary amount of separation. The above example is thus produced with the input

```
‘‘I regard computer typesetting as being
reasonably ‘straightforward’\,’’ he said.
```

2.6 Changing Fonts in Text Mode

LaTeX has numerous control sequences for changing the typestyle. The most useful of these is \emph{*text*} which *emphasises* some piece of text, setting it usually in an *italic font* (unless the surrounding text is already italicised). Thus, for example, the text

> The basic results and techniques of *Calculus* were discovered and developed by *Newton* and *Leibniz*, though many of the basic ideas can be traced to earlier work of *Cavalieri*, *Fermat*, *Barrow* and others.

is obtained by typing

```
The basic results and techniques of
\emph{Calculus} were discovered and developed
by \emph{Newton} and \emph{Leibniz}, though
many of the basic ideas can be traced to
earlier work of \emph{Cavalieri},
\emph{Fermat}, \emph{Barrow} and others.
```

There are other control sequences which italicise as well. The difference lies in the *semantic* or *functional* use of these commands, rather than the final output. `\emph` serves to indicate that the *reason* for the italics is to emphasise, whereas `\textit` (one of the other italics commands) serves the same semantic purpose as the italics button in Microsoft Word—that is, none at all. In order to keep to the 'mission' or governing principle of LaTeX that function is king, one should *never* use the purely cosmetic commands for italics when `\emph` is more suitable.

If the question of whether to use `\textit` and its fellows or `\emph` is unclear, the text should be read out loud, and if the word to be italicised is also stressed in the voice, it should be emphasised, not merely italicised.

A *font family* or *typeface* in LaTeX consists of a collection of related fonts characterized by *size*, *shape* and *series*. The font families available in LaTeX include roman, sans serif and `typewriter`. There are at least two ways to select a particular font: either with a so-called *tag* in the format `\textxx{`*text*`}`, or with a *declaration*, in the formats `\xx`, `\xxseries`, or `\xxshape`.

Declarations do not take an argument; rather, *everything* up until the end of the group is modified. Furthermore, *every* declaration has an environment of the same name.

- The LaTeX declarations `\rm` and `\rmfamily`, the environment `\begin{rmfamily}`... `\end{rmfamily}`, and the tag `\textrm{`*text*`}` typeset the specified text in Roman type. Computer Modern Roman features upright, *italic*, slanted, and SMALL CAPS shapes in both medium and **boldface** series.

- The LaTeX declarations `\sf` and `\sffamily`, the environment `\begin{sffamily}`... `\end{sffamily}`, and the tag `\textsf{`*text*`}` typeset the specified text in Grotesk type. Computer Modern Grotesk features upright and *slanted* shapes in both medium and boldface series.

- The LaTeX declarations `\tt` and `\ttfamily`, the environment `\begin{ttfamily}...\end{ttfamily}`, and the tag `\textrm{`*text*`}` typeset the specified text in monospaced Teletype type. Computer Modern Teletype features upright, *italic*, *slanted* and SMALL CAPS shapes, but there is no boldface series.

The *shape* of a font can be upright, *italic*, slanted or SMALL CAPS.

- The LaTeX declaration `\upshape`, the environment `\begin{ups` and the tag `\textup{`*text*`}` typeset the specified text with an upright shape: this is normally the default shape.

- *The LaTeX declarations* \itshape *and* \it, *the environment* \begin{itshape}.../\end{itshape}, *and the tag* \textit{text} *typeset the specified text with an italic shape.*

- The LaTeX declarations \slshape and \sl, the environment \begin{slshape}...\end{slshape}, and the tag \textsl{*text*} typeset the specified text with an oblique, or slanted shape: slanted text is midway between upright and italic.

- THE LATEX DECLARATIONS \scshape AND \sc, THE ENVIRONMENT \begin{scshape}...\end{scshape}, AND THE TAG \textsc{*text*} TYPESET THE SPECIFIED TEXT WITH A SMALL CAPS SHAPE IN WHICH ALL LETTERS ARE CAPITALS (WITH UPPERCASE LETTERS TALLER THAN LOWERCASE LETTERS).

The *series* of a font can be medium (the default) or **boldface:**

- The LaTeX declaration \mdseries, the environment \begin{mds and the tag \textmd{*text*} typeset the specified text with a medium series font.

- The LaTeX declarations \bfseries and \bf, the environment \begin{bfseries}.../\end{bfseries}, and the tag \textbf{*text*} typeset the specified text with a boldface series font.

At this point, it is worth noting that the two different types of declaration work differently from one another and from the tags. Most specifically, the declarations in the format \xx are atavisms (that is to say, relics) of original Plain TeX, and due attention should be given to their idiosyncracies. Using \bf, \it, and the others should be avoided especially when the document calls for font changes to be combined. The reason is that the old two-letter declarations clear LaTeX's internal font attributes and do not play nicely together. Case in point:

```
{\bf This should be in bold, {\rm this should
{\it space} correctly, and {\it this should be
in bold-italic}.  Pity it doesn't work that
way.}
```

When run through LaTeX, it produces this output:

> **This should be in bold,** this should *space* correctly, and *this should be in bold-italic*. Pity it doesn't work that way.

The native LaTeX declarations are better, but they, too, have a disadvantage. When changing from *italic* back to roman with a declaration, the computer will not insert additional space to compensate for the way some italic letters lean into the following character. It is necessary, therefore, to know how to use the so-called *italic correction* \/ Although judicious use of the italic correction may produce excellent spacing, it in a way defeats the purpose of LaTeX, in that the book designer was hired specifically so that the author would not have to speak directly to the typesetter. That having been said, however, the use of declarations can save a lot of time and is to be preferred in certain areas.

The use of italic correction is largely up to trial and error, except for the following advice: it is *never* to be used before a full stop. Notice the difference:

```
{\Huge
{\bf {\it half}hearted \\}
{\bfseries {\itshape half}hearted} \\
\textbf{\textit{half}hearted}} \\
```

*half*hearted
***half*hearted**
***half*hearted**

Text size in LaTeX is also flexible. LaTeX supports eleven different font sizes, which can be changed by the control sequences `\tiny`, `\scriptsize`, `\footnotesize`, `\small`, `\normalsize`, `\large`, `\Large`, `\LARGE`, `\huge`, `\Huge`, and `\HUGE`.

Font size can also be changed by means of environments (that is, by using, for example, `\begin{large}` and `\end{large}`).

Here is an example of changing font sizes:

> This normal-sized text is good for general purpose usage. However, some like things large, or perhaps larger, and even larger still. Freud, however, may have a few things to say if you insist on huge text. Many say that small is beautiful; but we can get smaller and smaller, tiny even.

which was produced by the code:

```
This normal-sized text is good for general
purpose usage.  However, some like things
{\large large}, or perhaps {\Large larger}, and
even {\LARGE larger still}. Freud, however, may
have a few things to say if you insist on
{\huge huge} text. Many say that {\small small}
is beautiful; but we can get {\footnotesize
smaller} and {\scriptsize smaller}, {\tiny
tiny} even.
```

2.7 Accents used in Text

There are a variety of control sequences for producing accents. For example, the control sequence `\'{o}` produces an *accent aigu* (acute accent) on the letter o. Thus typing

```
Sean Kennedy (Irish: Se\'{a}n \'{O}
Cinn\'{e}ide).
```

produces

> Sean Kennedy (Irish: Seán Ó Cinnéide).

Similarly, the control sequence `` \` `` is used to produce the *accent grave* in 'algèbre' and `\"`, to produce the *umlaut* in 'Universität' and the diæresis in 'coöperation'. Although the shapes of the diæresis and umlaut are the same, they are different accents: the umlaut is a sound shift, whereas the diæresis over-rides a digraph (two letters making one sound). The following table lists the accents supported by LaTeX in ordinary text:

\'{e}	é (*accent grave*)	e.g., math\'{e}matique yields 'mathé
\`{e}	è (*accent aigu*)	e.g., alg\`{e}bre yields 'algèbre'
\^{e}	ê (*circumflex*)	e.g., fen\^{e}tre yields 'fenêtre'
\"{e}	ë (*diæresis/umlaut*)	e.g., a\"{e}roplane yields 'aëroplane
\~{a}	ñ (*tilde*)	e.g., milh\~{a}o yields milhão'
\={\i}	ī (*macron*)	e.g., land\={\i}ca yields 'landīca'
\.{I}	İ (*tittle*)	e.g., \.{I}skilip yields 'İskilip'
\u{a}	ă (*breve*)	e.g., rom\^{a}n\u{a} yields 'română'
\v{c}	č (*háček*)	e.g., \v{C}ech yields 'Čech'
\H{o}	ő (*long umlaut*)	e.g., leveg\H{o} yields 'levegő'
\t{oo}	o͡o (*tie*)	
\c{c}	ç (*cedilla*)	e.g., Fran\c{c}ois yields 'François'
\d{o}	ọ (*dot below*)	
\b{o}	o̲ (*macron below*)	

These accents are for use in ordinary text. They cannot be used within mathematical formulæ, since different control sequences are used to produce so-called 'accents' within mathematics.

There are several other control sequences for English and foreign-language letters. The control sequences `\oe` and `\ae` produce the ligature œ and the letter æ (pronounced *ash*), used in many English words (like *subpœna* and *pædiatrician*). The control sequences `\i` and `\j` produce dotless 'ı' and 'ȷ'. These are required when placing an accent on the letter, as well as in the Turkish language, where *i* and *ı* produce different sounds. Thus, í is produced by typing `\'{\i}`, and the names of the cities İzmir and Diyarbakır by typing `\.{I}zmir` and `Diyarbak{\i}r`.

Symbol	*Control Sequence*	*Example*
œ, Œ	`\oe, \OE`	`f\oe tus` produces *fœtus*
æ, Æ	`\ae, \AE`	`formul\ae` produces *formulæ*
þ, Þ	`\th, \TH`	`\TH or` produces *Þor*
ð, Đ	`\dh, \DH`	`bor\dh um` produces *borðum*
ø, Ø	`\o, \O`	`s\o vn` produces *søvn*
å, Å	`\aa, \AA`	`riksm\aa l` produces *riksmå*
ß	`\ss`	`Stra\ss e` produces *Straße*
ł, Ł	`\l, \L`	`artyku\l` produces *artykuł*
đ, Đ	`\dj, \DJ`	`\dj akon` produces *đakon*
ŋ, Ŋ	`\ng, \NG`	`rea\ng gan` produces *reaŋga*

Using the default `T1` encoding, the letters *þ, ð, đ, and ŋ* are not available; therefore, if you plan to use them, there is a setting that will be discussed later.

In typesetting Icelandic, it is acceptable to use the accented ó (`\'{o}`) rather than ø (`\o`): both *sóvn* and *søvn* are correct. This is not the case in Færoese, as ó and ø are different letters. In Færoese, use ő (`\H{o}`) instead: for example, *østrogen* (`\o strogen`) or *őstrogen* (`\H{o}strogen`).

A space, or any other non-alphabetic character, must *always* be insertedafter an alphabetic control sequence; this space will not show up in the final output. If a space is *needed* after the symbol, there are several ways to do so (all of which will be established later), but the simplest is to force a space with the control sequence \␣ (a backstroke followed by a space).

2.8 Active Characters & Special Symbols in Text

The 'active characters'

```
# $ % & \ ^ _ { } ~
```

have special purposes within LaTeX. Thus they cannot be produced in the final document simply by typing them directly. On the rare occasions when one needs to use the special characters

$ % & _ { }

in the final document, they can be produced by typing the control sequences

```
\# \$ \% \& \_ \{ \}
```

respectively. On the other hand, the characters \, ^ and ~ cannot be produced simply by preceding them with a backslash. They can, however, be produced using `\textbackslash` (in text mode only), `\char94` and `\char126` respectively. (The decimal numbers 94 and 126 are the ASCII codes of these characters.)

Other special symbols can be introduced into text using the appropriate control sequences:

Symbol	*Control Sequence*
¿	`?‘`
¡	`!‘`
†	`\dag`
‡	`\ddag`
§	`\S`
¶	`\P`
©	`\copyright`
£	`\pounds`
ı	`\i`
ȷ	`\j`

2.9 Footnotes and Marginal Notes

In academic literature, it is important to ascertain the source, or provenance, of the facts and figures used therein. The contemporary method of citing sources, also called the Harvard method, is by setting them in brackets, but the more traditional alternative is with *footnotes*. Footnotes are the *only* choice when it comes to defining unfamiliar or non-standard nomenclature in technical documentation, or specifying parenthetical information. Therefore, footnotes are an integral feature of LaTeX documents.

To insert a footnote in LaTeX is easy: simply place the control sequence `\footnote` *directly* after the text to be cited or defined, with the text of the citation or definition immediately following and enclosed in braces {}. For example:

```
The conduct of a trial in England is undeniably
an impressive undertaking.  Costume alone
transports the viewer to Elizabethan times.
Counsel and judges, bewigged and
gowned,\footnote{Although wigs and gowns may
add dignity and solemnity to a British
courtroom, such costuming is not universally
accepted.} appear in a cloistered, regal
setting, strewn with leather-bound books.
Brightly coloured ribbons of red, green, yellow
and white, rather than metal clips and staples
fasten the legal papers.\footnote{The
differently coloured ribbons signify which side
counsel represents.}  After comparison with the
volatile atmosphere and often unruly conduct of
a trial in a United States courtroom, it is
natural to assume that the British model of
courtroom advocacy provides an instructive
model for its American
```

```
counterpart.\footnote{\textit{See} Maness v.\
Meyers, 419 U.S.\ 449 (1975); In re Dillinger,
461 F.2d 389 (7th Cir.\ 1972).}
```

produces

The conduct of a trial in England is undeniably an impressive undertaking. Costume alone transports the viewer to Elizabethan times. Counsel and judges, bewigged and gowned,[2] appear in a cloistered, regal setting, strewn with leather-bound books. Brightly coloured ribbons of red, green, yellow and white, rather than metal clips and staples fasten the legal papers.[3] After comparison with the volatile atmosphere and often unruly conduct of a trial in a United States courtroom, it is natural to assume that the British model of courtroom advocacy provides an instructive model for its American counterpart.[4]

[2]Although wigs and gowns may add dignity and solemnity to a British courtroom, such costuming is not universally accepted.

[3]The differently coloured ribbons signify which side counsel represents.

[4]*See* Maness v. Meyers, 419 U.S. 449 (1975); In re Dillinger, 461 F.2d 389 (7th Cir. 1972).

Similarly, marginal notes are generally used either to clarify unfamiliar terminology or to render a passage in simpler terms. They descended from the common practice of a reader or editor writing his own notes in the margin; as such, they have an additional role of serving as an *obelism*—a note from the proofreader or editor to the author, or between editors or authors.

Marginal notes can be set in either the left or the right margin. If the author does not specifically direct LaTeX as to into which margin the note goes, LaTeX will default to the right margin for one-sided layouts (such as articles) and to the outside margin for two-sided layouts (such as reports and books). The LaTeX control sequence to insert a marginal note in this fashion is `\marginpar`. For example, the input text:

```
Since the prices of factors are assumed to be
cheapest, the reason for the \marginpar{economy
of scale---specialisation \(\uparrow\) return}
initial decline in cost per unit must be that,
as the scale of the firm's production expands,
output increases at a faster rate than inputs.
Increasing returns may arise as a result of
increased opportunities for specialisation.
```

```
Alternatively, they arise because of factior
substitution made possible by mass production.
This implies economies of scale.

The expansion in output is proportionately less
than the expansion in input.  \marginpar{later
diseconomy of scale: output expansion \(<\)
input expansion \(\downarrow\) return}  The
implication is that the firm suffers
diseconomies of scale, such as control loss
in management.
```

produces

Since the prices of factors are assumed to be cheapest, the reason for the initial decline in cost per unit must be that, as the scale of the firm's production expands, output increases at a faster rate than inputs. Increasing returns may arise as a result of increased opportunities for specialisation. Alternatively, they arise because of factior substitution made possible by mass production. This implies economies of scale.

ecor of scal spec ↑ re

The expansion in output is proportionately less than the expansion in input. The implication is

later ecor of outp expa sion inpu pans ↓ re

> that the firm suffers diseconomies of scale, such as control loss in management.

To reverse the default behaviour, such that LaTeX inserts marginal notes on the *left* margin for one-sided layouts and on the *inside* margin for two-sided layouts, simply use the control sequence `\reversemarginpar`.

2.10 Commenting

There is a facility in LaTeX that permits writing text inside of a document without it appearing in the final output. Although this may seem counter-productive, it in fact opens up endless possibilities in book-writing. For instance: as an author, it may prove useful to keep a list of things to do. Or, being placed in the shoes of an editor, you may wish to enclose remarks on the author's writing. With this feature, known as 'comment markup', all this, and much more, is possible. To comment out a line, place the sign for per cent. (%) in front of it.

There is another use for the comment. Traditionally, each line in a text file must be no more than eighty characters (letters, numbers, and spaces) long. The carriage-return character is equivalent, in LaTeX input syntax, to a space. If a word needs to be split between two lines without leaving space between the two halves, a % sign can be placed before the end of the line, functionally commenting out the carriage-return.

For example,

```
This is an extra-%
ordinarily long sentence.
```

would produce:

This is an extra-ordinarily long sentence.

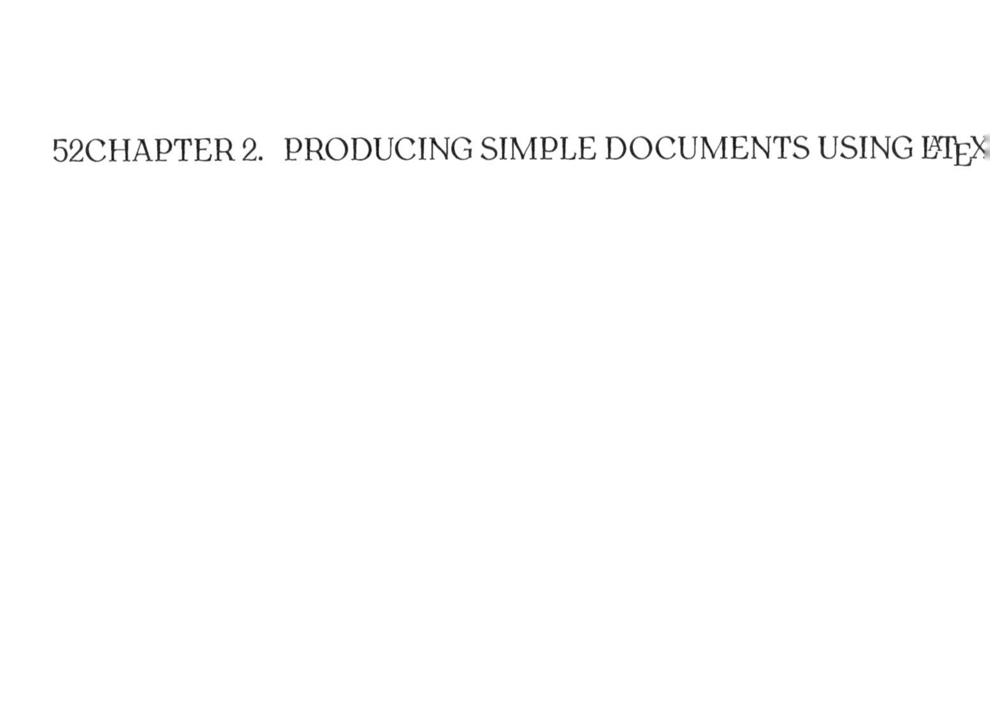

Chapter 3

Structure in LaTeX

3.1 The Structure of Text & Language

The main point of writing a text is to convey ideas, information, or knowledge to the reader. The reader will understand the text better if these ideas are well-structured, and will see and feel this structure much better if the typographical form reflects the logical and semantical structure of the content, hence the reason for the invention of LaTeX.

LaTeX is different from other typesetting systems in that the first (and usually only) thing one must tell it is the logical and semantical structure of a text. It then derives the typographical form of the text according to its internal rules (which are sometimes modified by accomplished LaTeX users known as TeXperts).

The most important text unit in LaTeX (and in typography) is the paragraph. In typography, it is called the 'text unit' because a paragraph is the typographical form that should reflect one coherent thought, or one idea. Therefore, if a new thought begins, a new paragraph should begin, and if not, only line breaks should be used. If in doubt about paragraph breaks, think about your text as a conveyor of ideas and thoughts. If you have a paragraph break, but the old thought continues, it should be made part of the same paragraph. If a new line of thought occurs in the same paragraph, then this new idea should be the subject of a new paragraph.

Most people completely underestimate the importance of well-placed breaks. Many people do not even know what the meaning of a paragraph break is, or, especially in LaTeX, introduce paragraph breaks without knowing it. The latter mistake is especially easy to make if equations are used in the text. Blank lines should always be placed either before a display equation **and** after it, or not be placed at all.

The next smaller text unit is a sentence. In English texts,

there is a larger space after a full stop that ends a sentence than after one that ends an abbreviation. LaTeX tries to figure out which one was intended. If LaTeX gets it wrong, it must be explicitly told what to do by means of the control sequence `\␣` (a backslash followed by a single space).

The convention of using a larger space after a full stop is not universally followed; some publishers observe so-called French spacing, in which the space following a full stop is equal in length to the space following a word. More specifically, English spacing uses a space one-third to one-half the width of the capital letter M for inter-word spacing, while it uses a space precisely the width of the capital letter M for inter-sentence spacing. In French spacing, both of these are identical.

To use French spacing, the control sequence `\frenchspacing` may be employed before the text that is so to be spaced; the confusingly-named `\nonfrenchspacing` reverts to English spacing. For example:

```
\frenchspacing
Upon entering a set of barrister's chambers,
one cannot help but notice the pervasive quiet
and orderliness. The telephone rarely rings in
a barrister's room.  It may ring, sometimes
```

```
frantically, but it is in the barrister's
clerk's room.  Instead, one is greeted by a
cloistered, albeit crowded, atmosphere.
Rather, it is the solicitors whose offices more
closely resemble those of the American
attorney: telephones constantly ringing,
telephone messages accumulating, clients and
witnesses waiting in the reception room, stacks
of books, pleadings and papers overflowing the
desk, bookcases and cabinets.

\nonfrenchspacing
One of the unique features of each set of
chambers is the mandatory employment of a
clerk, who manages every aspect of a
barrister's professional life: the distribution
of work, arrangement of the calendar, state of
the books, and the negotiation and collection
of fees.  The close barrister-clerk
relationship is reflected in the manner in
which barristers acquire their work. Solicitors
refer cases to a barrister of their choice by
contacting the barrister's clerk.  If the
barrister is available and an acceptable fee is
```

```
negotiated by the solicitor and clerk on behalf
of the barrister, the solicitor sends a brief
to chambers.
```

produces

Upon entering a set of barrister's chambers, one cannot help but notice the pervasive quiet and orderliness. The telephone rarely rings in a barrister's room. It may ring, sometimes frantically, but it is in the barrister's clerk's room. Instead, one is greeted by a cloistered, albeit crowded, atmosphere. Rather, it is the solicitors whose offices more closely resemble those of the American attorney: telephones constantly ringing, telephone messages accumulating, clients and witnesses waiting in the reception room, stacks of books, pleadings and papers overflowing the desk, bookcases and cabinets.

One of the unique features of each set of chambers is the mandatory employment of a clerk, who manages every aspect of a barrister's professional life: the distribution of work, arrangement of the calendar, state of the books, and

> the negotiation and collection of fees. The close barrister-clerk relationship is reflected in the manner in which barristers acquire their work. Solicitors refer cases to a barrister of their choice by contacting the barrister's clerk. If the barrister is available and an acceptable fee is negotiated by the solicitor and clerk on behalf of the barrister, the solicitor sends a brief to chambers.

The structuring of text extends even to parts of sentences. Most languages have very complex punctuation rules, but in many languages (including German and English), you will get almost every comma right if you remember what it represents: a short stop in the flow of language. If you are not sure about where to put a comma, read the sentence aloud and take a short breath at every comma. If this feels awkward at some place, delete that comma; if you feel the urge to breathe (or make a short stop) at some other place, insert a comma.

Finally, the paragraphs of a text should also be structured logically at a higher level, by putting them into chapters, sections, subsections, and so on. This is, of course, accomplished by typing the relevant control sequences.

3.2 Logical Headings in LaTeX

To divide text, LaTeX uses a system of logical headings; these are analogous to logical HTML headings one through seven, in that no formatting is needed, or, indeed, possible—LaTeX automatically formats each heading according to its internal instructions and with perfect consistency. Most types, or *classes* of document, support six types of heading; in order from top to bottom, the control sequences to insert them are `\part`, `\section`,`\subsection` and `\subsubsection`. LaTeX will number the sections and subsections automatically. The title of the section should be surrounded by curly brackets and placed immediately after the relevant control sequence. When processed by LaTeX, the input

```
\part{Hierarchy of \LaTeX{} Documents}
\section{Section Headings}

We explain in this section how to obtain
headings for the various sections and
subsections of our document.

\subsection{Headings in the ‘article’ Document
            Style}
```

```
In the 'article' style, the document may be
divided up into parts, sections, subsections
and subsubsections, and each can be given a
title, printed in a boldface font, simply by
issuing the appropriate control sequence.

\subsection{Numbering of Headings}
In the 'article' style, parts, sections,
subsections, and subsubsections are all
numbered.
```

will create four headings (for a part, section, subsection and subsubsection) in large **bold** font, and properly numbered. Parts are numbered in capital Roman numerals (*i.e.* I, II, III, IV), while sections and subsections use Arabic numerals. Subsubsections are numbered (again, using Arabic numerals) only in articles; books and reports written in LaTeX do not use numbered subsubsections.

Sometimes the automatic numbering provided by LaTeX needs to be suppressed; specifically, this is most often done for forewords, introductions, preambles, afterwords, and acknowledgements. This can be done by placing an asterisk before the title of the section or subsection. Thus, for example, the section numbers in the above example could be suppressed by typing

```
\section*{Section Headings}

We explain in this section how to obtain
headings for the various sections and
subsections of our document.

\subsection*{Headings in the ‘article’ Document
             Style}

In the ‘article’ style, the document may be
divided up into sections, subsections and
subsubsections, and each can be given a title,
printed in a boldface font, simply by issuing
the appropriate control sequence.
```

LaTeX also provides paragraph and subparagraph headings, although they are a misnomer: both of these support multiple paragraphs. Their use is, for the most part, identical to that of parts, sections, subsections, and subsubsections, but for the single *caveat* that only *one* line break should be inserted after the heading. For example, the following source text:

```
\paragraph{Note}
Books and reports in \LaTeX{} have one
additional hierarchical heading: the
\textit{chapter}.  Appropriately enough, the
control sequence to begin a chapter is
\verb/\chapter/ and they are numbered with the
word \textit{Chapter} and an Arabic numeral.

\paragraph{Numbering}
The numbering system is different in books and
reports, as well.  Since the second level of
heading is now the \emph{chapter} rather than
the section, the numbering changes to reflect
this. Chapters now take a single Arabic number,
sections take two numbers delimited by a full
stop, and subsections take three numbers also
delimited by a full stop.  Subsubsections lose
their numbering.
```

produces the output:

Note Books and reports in LaTeX have one additional hierarchical heading: the *chapter*. Appropriately enough, the control sequence to begin a chapter is `\chapter` and they are numbered with the word *Chapter* and an Arabic numeral. The numbering system is different in books and reports, as well. Since the second level of heading is now the *chapter* rather than the section, the numbering changes to reflect this. Chapters now take a single Arabic number, sections take two numbers delimited by a full stop, and subsections take three numbers also delimited by a full stop. Subsubsections lose their numbering.

Note The entire previous chapter does not apply to *letters* and *slides* decks written in LaTeX. Sectioning commands in letters and slides are entirely different and will be covered in further sections.

3.3 Line Breaking and Page Breaking

Books are often typeset with each line having the same length. LaTeX inserts the necessary line breaks and spaces between words by optimizing the contents of a whole paragraph. If necessary, it also hyphenates words that would not fit comfortably on a line. How the paragraphs are typeset depends on the document class. Normally the first line of a paragraph is indented, and there is no additional space between two paragraphs.

In special cases it might be necessary to order LaTeX to break a line: `\bs` or `\newline` starts a new line without starting a new paragraph; additionally, `\bs*` prohibits a page break after the forced line break. Similarly, `\newpage` starts a new page.

```
\linebreak[n]
\nolinebreak[n]
\pagebreak[n]
\nopagebreak[n]
```

suggest places where a break may (or may not) happen. They enable the author to influence their actions with the optional argument *n*, which can be set to a number between zero and four. If *n* is set to a value below 4, LaTeX is given the option of ignoring the control sequence if the result would look ugly; *i.e.*, this is a request, not a command.

LaTeX always tries to produce the best line breaks possible. If it cannot find a way to break the lines in a manner that meets its high standards, it lets one line protrude on the right of the paragraph. LaTeX then informs the user by logging a statement of `overfull hbox` while processing the input file. This happens most often when LaTeX cannot find a suitable place to hyphenate a word. Although LaTeX types out a warning when that happens and displays the offending line, such lines are not always easy to find. If the option `draft` is used in the `\documentclass` control sequence, these lines will be marked with a thick black line (pejoratively called a slug) on the right margin.

LaTeX can be 'told' to lower its standards a little by means of the `\sloppy` control sequence. It prevents such over-long lines by increasing the inter-word spacing—even if it does not consider the final output optimal. In this case, a warning of an `underfull hbox` is given to the user. In most such cases, the result looks poor. The control sequence `\fussy` brings LaTeX back to its default behaviour.

3.4 Tags, Declarations, and Environments

Broadly speaking, there are three kinds of control sequence in LaTeX:

1. environments;
2. declarations; and
3. tags.

Control sequences in the format `\begin{blah}` and `\end{blah}` are known as *environments*. Whatever text is within the environment is subject to certain rules; there are environments named `letter`, `itemize`, `enumerate`, and `tabular`: each of them sets certain rules for the text contained therein, and typesets it a certain way. Every environment has an associated `\begin` and `\end` statement, and text in every environment must be enclosed in these statements. Environments may be nested arbitrarily, which provides LaTeX with its hierarchy; however, they must *never* overlap. The following

```
\begin{blah}
```

```
\begin{bleurgh}
\end{blah}
\end{bleurgh}
```

is nonsense; the (entirely hypothetical) `bleurgh` environment is halfway inside of the `blah` environment, and halfway outside of it. When encountering this series of environments, LaTeX will issue an error and cease functioning.

Other control sequences—these are known as *tags*—take *arguments*. An argument specifies information a control sequence may or must have in order to make sense. For instance, making text bold would be meaningless unless there was, in fact, text to make bold. Each mandatory argument is surrounded by braces ({ and }); each optional argument, by brackets ([and]).

Braces are also used for *grouping* purposes; there is no limit to the level of grouping, as long as there are as many opened as there are closed. The purpose of grouping is to segregate sections of text that may need to be altered independently with LaTeX commands. Everything in one group is treated the same way, and there are control sequences that apply until the end of the group (environments are a type of group). The group itself is invisible on paper unless it is used for something. For instance:

```
This {sentence} is composed of {{{m}{a}{n}{y}}
{groups and {subgroups}}.} This sentence
contains{} a null group.
```

outputs:

> This sentence is composed of many groups and subgroups. This sentence contains a null group.

The null group {} is used for spacing: for instance, all the space after a control sequence is swallowed up, unless the control sequence is followed by a null group. In mathematics mode, superscripts and subscripts occur on top of each other by default; if the intent is to have them one after the other, this can be done with a null group.

Declarations are control sequences that modify text until the end of a group; they take no argument and are usually somewhat short in length. For instance:

```
{The \it second \rm word in this sentence has
been italicised by means of a declaration; so
has \it this \rm one. On the other hand,
\textit{these three words} have been italicised
via the \verb/\textit/ command.}
```

produces

> The *second* word in this sentence has been italicised by means of a declaration; so has *this* one. On the other hand, *these three words* have been italicised via the `\textit` command.

3.5 Title and Author

No matter whether typesetting a romantic novel or an academic thesis that could change the course of history, each significant piece of written work requires a title; in most cases, the author will also want credit, and, in non-fictional works, a date is also not unimportant. LaTeX makes it almost trivially simple to include this most basic of information—as it should.

Unlike with a word-processing package, title pages are always of a professional standard when using LaTeX. Just as with other information, the computer takes care of layout, font, and placement; the user merely has to supply the requisite information.

All of the various document classes supported by LaTeX handle the title in different ways; the `article` class, just like articles in a magazine, will handle a title differently compared to a report or book of the same name. LaTeX's handling of a title will always be appropriate to the document class in question.

Including a title, author's name, and date in the document is simple. The most rudimentary example would be as follows:

```
\documentclass{article}
\title{De Conceptione ac Graviditate
Tubo-uterina, sive Interstitiale}
\author{A.\ Sacconi, M.D.}
\date{21 September, 1891}
\begin{document}
\maketitle
...
\end{document}
```

If the \date tag is omitted, or a date field of \today is entered, the date on the title page will be automatically updated to reflect the date the document was compiled.

Many articles and books, especially in technical fields, have two or more authors. In that case, they may be listed side-by-side, with the \and declaration between them:

```
\documentclass{article}
\title{Can Quantum-Mechanical Description of
Physical Reality Be Considered Complete?}
\author{Albert Einstein \and Boris Podolsky
\and Nathan Rosen}
\date{25 March, 1935}
\begin{document}
\maketitle
...
\end{document}
```

To put the authors' names below, rather than beside, each other is simply a matter of replacing the \and control sequence with \\.

In academic journals, it is common practice to include not only the authors' names, as in the two preceding examples, but also their addresses or affiliations. In those cases, the \\ declaration is invaluable; although LaTeX is a useful programme, it does not know that addresses are meant to be on separate lines. An example of a more complex title:

```
\documentclass{article}
\title{Action integrals and partition functions
      in quantum gravity}
```

```
\author{Gary W. Gibbons \\
        Max-Planck-Institute f\"{u}r Physik und
        Astrophysik \\
        8 M\"{u}nchen 40 \\
        Postfach 401212 \\
        Bundesrepublik Deutschland \and
        Stephen W. Hawking \\
        Department of Applied Mathematics and
        Theoretical Physics \\
        University of Cambridge \\
        England}
\date{4 October, 1976}
\begin{document}
\maketitle
...
\end{document}
```

3.6 Abstracts

In academia, and in journals most especially, it is common practice to include a short summary, or abstract, of the work in question. Research reports, whether commercial, governmental, or academic, also tend to follow this custom. The reason for the tradition is that research is a time-sensitive field, with often impenetrable reports that must be carefully studied to glean important information. By the time the reader wades through the methodology and the analysis, and finally gets to the conclusion, valuable time might have passed.

As a software package built specifically for the academic arena (although useful in all the professions), LaTeX supports abstracts. As with other text that merits special treatment, there is an `abstract` environment, to be inserted directly after `\maketitle` if the work has a title, and after `\begin{document}` if it does not. For example:

```
\documentclass{article}
\title{Action integrals and partition functions
       in quantum gravity}
\author{Gary W. Gibbons \\
        Max-Planck-Institute f\"{u}r Physik und
        Astrophysik \\
        8 M\"{u}nchen 40 \\
        Postfach 401212 \\
        Bundesrepublik Deutschland \and
        Stephen W. Hawking \\
        Department of Applied Mathematics and
```

```
        Theoretical Physics \\
        University of Cambridge \\
        England}
\date{4 October, 1976}
\begin{document}
\maketitle
\begin{abstract}
One can evaluate the action for a gravitational
field on a section of the complexified
spacetime which avoids the singularities. In
this manner we obtain finite, purely imaginary
values for the actions of the Kerr-Newman
solutions and de Sitter space. One
interpretation of these values is that they
give the probabilities for finding such metrics
in the vacuum state. Another interpretation is
that they give the contribution of that metric
to the partition function for a grand canonical
ensemble at a certain temperature, angular
momentum, and charge. We use this approach to
evaluate the entropy of these metrics and find
that it is always equal to one quarter the area
of the event horizon in fundamental units. This
agrees with previous derivations by completely
```

```
different methods. In the case of a stationary
system such as a star with no event horizon,
the gravitational field has no entropy.
\end{abstract}
...
\end{document}
```

Unless told otherwise, LaTeX will use the word 'Abstract' as the heading. If different terminology ('Summary', for instance) is required, the control sequence `\renewcommand` needs to be used as follows:

```
\documentclass{report}
\title{``Never Apologize'': PM Harper's
       Governing Style}
\author{David Wilkins}
\date{27 June, 2008}
\begin{document}
\maketitle
\renewcommand{\abstractname}{Summary}
\begin{abstract}
Prime Minister Stephen Harper's reputation as a
master political strategist is somewhat
tattered in the wake of November's stunning
```

```
near-fatal mis-step to abolish public financing
for all political parties. However, at least
on the surface, he remains unbowed and
unapologetic. Relying on an extremely small
circle of advisors and his own instincts, he
has played the game of high-stakes, partisan
politics well, but his reputation for
decisiveness and shrewdness has been tarnished
by a sometimes vindictive pettiness. With only
a few exceptions, he has not built the bridges
to the opposition typical of a minority PM.
Moving from surpluses to deficits, he will face
new imperatives in the changed economic and
political landscape of 2009 to adopt a more
conciliatory and inclusive approach. However,
this will go against the grain for such an
instinctively combative Prime Minister.
\end{abstract}
...
\end{document}
```

The further use of the \renewcommand control sequence will be elucidated later in this guide.

3.7 Alignment

LaTeX aligns text with the margin in four different ways: left alignment, right alignment, centre, and justification. Justification is the default setting; whenever one of the other alignments is not enabled, the text will be fully justified. In full justification, the text is flush with both the left and right margins: the length of inter-word spacing is adjusted to compensate.

Left alignment is comparable to the output of a typewriter or a word processor: the left edge of the text is flush with the margin, while the right edge is left ragged. The commands `\begin{flushleft}` and `\end{flushleft}` align the text to the left. The following is an example of left-aligned text:

```
\begin{flushleft}
It is not so much affirmed as taken for
granted, by all who ever mention opium,
formally or incidentally, that it does or can
produce intoxication.  Now, reader, assure
yourself, {\it meo perieulo}, that no quantity
of opium ever did or could intoxicate.  As to
the tincture of opium (commonly called
```

```
laudanum) {\it that} might certainly intoxicate
if a man could bear to take enough of it; but
why? Because it contains so much proof spirit,
and not because it contains so much opium. But
crude opium, I affirm peremptorily, is
incapable of producing any state of body at all
resembling that which is produced by alcohol,
and not in {\it degree} only incapable, but
even in {\it kind}: it is not in the quantity
of its effects merely, but in the quality, that
it differs altogether.\footnote{Taken from {\it
Confessions of an Opium Eater}, Thos de
Quincey, 1821}
\end{flushleft}
```

When passed through LaTeX, it produces

It is not so much affirmed as taken for granted,
by all who ever mention opium, formally or
incidentally, that it does or can produce
intoxication. Now, reader, assure yourself, *meo
perieulo*, that no quantity of opium ever did or
could intoxicate. As to the tincture of opium
(commonly called laudanum) *that* might

> certainly intoxicate if a man could bear to take enough of it; but why? Because it contains so much proof spirit, and not because it contains so much opium. But crude opium, I affirm peremptorily, is incapable of producing any state of body at all resembling that which is produced by alcohol, and not in *degree* only incapable, but even in *kind*: it is not in the quantity of its effects merely, but in the quality, that it differs altogether.[1]

Right alignment is precisely the opposite: the left edge is left ragged, while the right edge is made flush. This is the most common alignment (other than full justification) in languages that read right-to-left, such as Arabic and Hebrew. In English, right alignment is often used when printing tables of data, for example. The commands `\begin{flushright}` and `\end{flushright}` align text to the right. For example, entering

```
\begin{flushright}
But the main distinction lies in this, that
whereas wine disorders the mental faculties,
```

[1]Taken from *Confessions of an Opium Eater*, Thos de Quincey, 1821

```
opium, on the contrary (if taken in a proper
manner), introduces amongst them the most
exquisite order, legislation, and harmony.
Wine robs a man of his self-possession; opium
greatly invigorates it.  Wine unsettles and
clouds the judgement, and gives a preternatural
brightness and a vivid exaltation to the
contempts and the admirations, the loves and
the hatreds of the drinker; opium, on the
contrary, communicates serenity and equipoise
to all the faculties, active or passive, and
with respect to the temper and moral feelings
in general it gives simply that sort of vital
warmth which is approved by the judgment, and
which would probably always accompany a bodily
constitution of prim\ae val or antediluvian
health. \footnote{de Quincey, 1821}
\end{flushright}
```

produces

But the main distinction lies in this, that
whereas wine disorders the mental faculties,
opium, on the contrary (if taken in a proper

manner), introduces amongst them the most exquisite order, legislation, and harmony. Wine robs a man of his self-possession; opium greatly invigorates it. Wine unsettles and clouds the judgement, and gives a preternatural brightness and a vivid exaltation to the contempts and the admirations, the loves and the hatreds of the drinker; opium, on the contrary, communicates serenity and equipoise to all the faculties, active or passive, and with respect to the temper and moral feelings in general it gives simply that sort of vital warmth which is approved by the judgment, and which would probably always accompany a bodily constitution of primæval or antediluvian health. [2]

Finally, text can also be centred, or aligned along the centre-line of the page. This alignment is often used for the title of a work, as well as for the lyrics of a song or a poem. It is not advised to centre a body of text made up of multiple lines, because it is considered less legible: the ragged starting edges make it more difficult for the reader to track from

[2] de Quincey, 1821

one line to the next. The LaTeX commands \begin{center} and \end{center} (note the American spelling) centre text. Disregarding the advice given above, this example of centred text

```
\begin{center}
Thus, for instance, opium, like wine, gives an
expansion to the heart and the benevolent
affections; but then, with this remarkable
difference, that in the sudden development of
kind-heartedness which accompanies inebriation
there is always more or less of a maudlin
character, which exposes it to the contempt of
the bystander.  Men shake hands, swear eternal
friendship, and shed tears, no mortal knows
why; and the sensual creature is clearly
uppermost.  But the expansion of the benigner
feelings incident to opium is no febrile
access, but a healthy restoration to that state
which the mind would naturally recover upon the
removal of any deep-seated irritation of pain
that had disturbed and quarrelled with the
impulses of a heart originally just and good.
\footnote{de Quincey, 1821}
```

```
\end{center}
```

produces

Thus, for instance, opium, like wine, gives an expansion to the heart and the benevolent affections; but then, with this remarkable difference, that in the sudden development of kind-heartedness which accompanies inebriation there is always more or less of a maudlin character, which exposes it to the contempt of the bystander. Men shake hands, swear eternal friendship, and shed tears, no mortal knows why; and the sensual creature is clearly uppermost. But the expansion of the benigner feelings incident to opium is no febrile access, but a healthy restoration to that state which the mind would naturally recover upon the removal of any deep-seated irritation of pain that had disturbed and quarrelled with the impulses of a heart originally just and good. [3]

[3]de Quincey, 1821

3.8 Lists

LaTeX provides the following list environments:

- `enumerate` for numbered lists,
- `itemize` for non-numbered lists,
- `description` for description lists

The items in a *numbered* list should be enclosed between

`\begin{enumerate}` and `\end{enumerate}`

and should each be preceded by the control sequence `\item` (which will automatically generate the number labelling the item). For example, the text

> A *metric space* (X, d) consists of a set X on which is defined a *distance function* which assigns to each pair of points of X a distance between them, and which satisfies the following four axioms:
>
> 1. $d(x, y) \geq 0$ for all points x and y of X;

2. $d(x,y) = d(y,x)$ for all points x and y of X;
3. $d(x,z) \leq d(x,y) + d(y,z)$ for all points x, y and z of X;
4. $d(x,y) = 0$ if and only if the points x and y coincide.

is generated by LaTeX from the following input:

```
A \emph{metric space} \((X,d)\) consists of a
set~\(X\) on which is defined a \emph{distance
function} which assigns to each pair of points
of \(X\) a distance between them, and which
satisfies the following four axioms:

\begin{enumerate}
\item \(d(x,y) \geq 0\) for all points \(x\)
and \(y\) of \(X\);
\item \(d(x,y) = d(y,x)\) for all points \(x\)
and \(y\) of \(X\);
\item \(d(x,z) \leq d(x,y) + d(y,z)\) for all
points \(x\), \(y\) and \(z\) of \(X\);
\item \(d(x,y) = 0\) if and only if the points
\(x\) and \(y\) coincide.
\end{enumerate}
```

If we replace

`\begin{enumerate}` and `\end{enumerate}`

in the above input by

`\begin{itemize}` and `\end{itemize}`

respectively, LaTeX generates an itemized list in which each item is preceeded by a 'bullet':

> A *metric space* (X, d) consists of a set X on which is defined a *distance function* which assigns to each pair of points of X a distance between them, and which satisfies the following four axioms:
>
> - $d(x, y) \geq 0$ for all points x and y of X;
> - $d(x, y) = d(y, x)$ for all points x and y of X;
> - $d(x, z) \leq d(x, y) + d(y, z)$ for all points x, y and z of X;
> - $d(x, y) = 0$ if and only if the points x and y coincide.

Description lists (for glossaries etc.) are produced using

`\begin{description} ... \end{description}`

The items in the list should be enclosed between

`\begin{description}` and `\end{description}`

and should each be preceded by `\item[`*label*`]`, where *label* is the label to be assigned to each item. For example, the text

> We now list the definitions of *open ball, open set* and *closed set* in a metric space.
>
> **open ball** The *open ball* of radius r about any point x is the set of all points of the metric space whose distance from x is strictly less than r;
>
> **open set** A subset of a metric space is an *open set* if, given any point of the set, some open ball of sufficiently small radius about that point is contained wholly within the set;
>
> **closed set** A subset of a metric space is a *closed set* if its complement is an open set.

is generated by LaTeX from the following input:

```
We now list the definitions of \emph{open
ball}, \emph{open set} and \emph{closed set} in
a metric space.
\begin{description}
\item[open ball]
The \emph{open ball} of radius~\(r\) about any
point~\(x\) is the set of all points of the
metric space whose distance from \(x\) is
strictly less than \(r\);
\item[open set]
A subset of a metric space is an \emph{open
set} if, given any point of the set, some open
ball of sufficiently small radius about that
point is contained wholly within the set;
\item[closed set]
A subset of a metric space is a \emph{closed
set} if its complement is an open set.
\end{description}
```

3.9 Displayed Quotations

Displayed quotations can be embedded in text using the `quote` and `quotation` environments

```
\begin{quote} ... \end{quote}
```

and

```
\begin{quotation} ... \end{quotation}.
```

The `quote` environment is recommended for short quotations: the whole quotation is indended in the `quote` environment, but the first lines of individual paragraphs are not further indented. The input file

```
Isaac Newton discovered the basic techiques of
the calculus of fluxions and fluents, and
applied them in the study of many problems in
mathematical physics.  His main mathematical
works are the \emph{Principia} and the
\emph{Optics}.  He summarised his own estimate
of his work as follows:

\begin{quote}
I do not know what I may appear to the world;
but to myself I seem to have been only like a
boy, playing on the sea-shore, and diverting
myself, in now and then finding a smoother
```

```
pebble, or a prettier shell than ordinary,
whilst the great ocean of truth lay all
undiscovered before me.
\end{quote}

In later years Newton became embroiled in a
bitter priority dispute with Leibniz over the
discovery of the basic techniques of calculus.
```

is typeset by LaTeX as follows:

> Isaac Newton discovered the basic techiques of the calculus of fluxions and fluents, and applied them in the study of many problems in mathematical physics. His main mathematical works are the *Principia* and the *Optics*. He summarised his own estimate of his work as follows:
>
> > I do not know what I may appear to the world; but to myself I seem to have been only like a boy, playing on the seashore, and diverting myself, in now and then finding a smoother pebble, or a prettier shell than ordinary, whilst the

> great ocean of truth lay all undiscovered before me.
>
> In later years Newton became embroiled in a bitter priority dispute with Leibniz over the discovery of the basic techniques of calculus.

For longer quotations one may use the **quotation** environment: the whole quotation is indented, and the openings of paragraphs are then further indented in the normal fashion.

3.10 Verse

In the humanities, writing any academic document often requires the typesetting of verse; this is all the more true in languages with a strong poetic tradition, and the English language has one of the strongest poetic traditions of them all. To this end, LaTeX includes the `verse` environment.

Using the `verse` environment is surprisingly easy. The text to be set as verse is inserted between the control sequences `\begin{verse}` and `\end{verse}`, with manual line breaks (`\\`) at the end of every line.

For instance, the code

```
\begin{verse}
``Forward, the Light Brigade!''\\
Was there a man dismay'd?\\
Not tho' the soldier knew\\
Someone had blunder'd:\\
Theirs not to make reply,\\
Theirs not to reason why,\\
Theirs but to do and die:\\
Into the valley of Death\\
Rode the six hundred.\\
\end{verse}
```

produces

> "Forward, the Light Brigade!"
> Was there a man dismay'd?
> Not tho' the soldier knew
> Someone had blunder'd:
> Theirs not to make reply,
> Theirs not to reason why,
> Theirs but to do and die:
> Into the valley of Death
> Rode the six hundred.

3.11 Prepared Text

It is sometimes necessary in LaTeX to produce and format *prepared text*. Prepared text, for the purposes of this manual, is defined as text to be printed as-is, without regards to LaTeX spacing rules or so-called active characters.

Examples of prepared text include computer programming code, as well as space-delimited tables (that is, using only tabs and spaces). In this latter case, however, it is far preferable to reformat the table to use LaTeX syntax.

To typeset prepared text, LaTeX includes a facility known as *verbatim mode*. There are several variations on this feature; exactly which variation to use depends, among other things, on the length and desired placement of said text.

The `\verb` control sequence is best used when inserting only a short segment of prepared text, such as a single computer command. Note that this control sequence uses a unique syntax for delimiting its range (*i.e.*, its argument). Because many programming languages commonly use braces `{}` in their syntaxes, LaTeX can not use them as boundary markers. Instead, the argument of the `\verb` control sequence is bounded by *any* two identical non-alphabetic characters, with the exception of the asterisk (*) and the backslash (\).

For example, the commands `\verb@blah{}@`, `\verb|blah{}|`, and `\verb/blah{}/` are all valid, but `\verb{blah}` is not, because the delimiters don't match. Delimiters must be chosen with care: the delimiter must *not* be used inside the command itself. The three valid examples all produce the string `blah{}`, in `teletype font` inline with the surrounding text.

If the string is one in which the presence of whitespace is significant, use the `\verb*` control sequence. It works precisely the same as `\verb`, but renders spaces as ␣, and tabs as .

For larger tracts of prepared text, use the `verbatim` environment. Like all LaTeX environments, everything between the `\start{verbatim}` and `\end{verbatim}` is treated according to specific rules. In this particular case, the text is displayed in a separate paragraph and set in teletype font. Furthermore, and perhaps most importantly, LaTeX disregards all control sequences and active characters therewithin.

Again, to emphasise whitespace, the `verbatim*` environment may be used instead. Like the `\verb*` control sequence, it makes spaces visible; like the `verbatim` environment, it displays the text separately, in its own paragraph. Note the difference:

```
C AREA OF A TRIANGLE - HERON'S FORMULA
```

```
C INPUT - CARD READER UNIT 5, INTEGER INPUT
C OUTPUT - LINE PRINTER UNIT 6, REAL OUTPUT
C INPUT ERROR DISPAY ERROR OUTPUT CODE 1 IN JOB CONTI
      INTEGER A,B,C
      READ(5,501) A,B,C
501   FORMAT(3I5)
      IF(A.EQ.0 .OR. B.EQ.0 .OR. C.EQ.0) STOP 1
      S = (A + B + C) / 2.0
      AREA = SQRT( S * (S - A) * (S - B) * (S - C))
      WRITE(6,601) A,B,C,AREA
601   FORMAT(4H A= ,I5,5H  B= ,I5,5H  C= ,I5,8H  AREA
      STOP
      END
```

```
␣␣␣␣␣␣INTEGER␣A,B,C
␣␣␣␣␣␣READ(5,501)␣A,B,C
501␣␣␣FORMAT(3I5)
␣␣␣␣␣␣IF(A.EQ.0␣.OR.␣B.EQ.0␣.OR.␣C.EQ.0)␣STOP␣1
␣␣␣␣␣␣S␣=␣(A␣+␣B␣+␣C)␣/␣2.0
␣␣␣␣␣␣AREA␣=␣SQRT(␣S␣*␣(S␣-␣A)␣*␣(S␣-␣B)␣*␣(S␣-␣C))
␣␣␣␣␣␣WRITE(6,601)␣A,B,C,AREA
601␣␣␣FORMAT(4H␣A=␣,I5,5H␣␣B=␣,I5,5H␣␣C=␣,I5,8H␣␣AREA
␣␣␣␣␣␣STOP
␣␣␣␣␣␣END
```

3.12 Tables

Tables can be produced in LaTeX using the `tabular` environment. For example, the text

> The first five International Congresses of Mathematicians were held in the following cities:
>
> | | | |
> |---|---|---|
> | Chicago | U.S.A. | 1893 |
> | Zürich | Switzerland | 1897 |
> | Paris | France | 1900 |
> | Heidelberg | Germany | 1904 |
> | Rome | Italy | 1908 |

is produced in LaTeX using the following input file:

```
The first five International Congresses of
Mathematicians were held in the following
cities:
\begin{quote}
\begin{tabular}{lll}
Chicago&U.S.A.&1893\\
Z\"{u}rich&Switzerland&1897\\
Paris&France&1900\\
Heidelberg&Germany&1904\\
Rome&Italy&1908
```

```
\end{tabular}
\end{quote}
```

The `\begin{tabular}` control sequence must be followed by a string of characters enclosed within braces which specifies the format of the table. In the above example, the string `{lll}` is a format specification for a table with three columns of left-justified text. Within the body of the table the ampersand character `&` is used to separate columns of text within each row, and the double backslash `\\` is used to separate the rows of the table.

The next example shows how to obtain a table with vertical and horizontal lines. The text

Ammunition		
Calibre	Description	Price ($)
Beehive	100 pieces	6.25
	8 oz.	12.00
	3 lbs.	48.50
10 AWG	20 pieces	11.35
	50 pieces	22.75
	100 pieces	40.00
Nagant	each	1.99

is produced in LaTeX using the following input file:

```
\begin{tabular}{ll|r}
\multicolumn{2}{c}{Ammunition} & \\
\cline{1-2}
Calibre & Description & Price (\$) \\
\hline
Beehive & 100 pieces  & 6.25 \\
        & 8 oz.       & 12.00 \\
        & 3 lbs.      & 48.50 \\
10 AWG  & 20 pieces   & 11.35 \\
        & 50 pieces   & 22.75 \\
        & 100 pieces  & 40.00 \\
Nagant  & each        &  1.99 \\
\end{tabular}
```

In a `tabular` environment, the format specification after `\begin{tabular}` should consist of one or more of the following, enclosed within braces { and }:

`l`	specifies a column of left-justified text
`c`	specifies a column of centred text
`r`	specifies a column of right-justified text
`p{`*width*`}`	specifies a left-justified column of the given wid
|	inserts a vertical line between columns
`@{`*text*`}`	inserts the given *text* between columns

A string *str* of characters in the format specification can be repeated *num* times using the construction *{*num*}{*str*}. For example, a table with 15 columns of right-justified text enclosed within vertical lines can be produced using the format specification `{|*{15}{r|}}`.

If additional vertical space is required between rows of the table, then this can be produced by specifying the amount of space within square brackets after \\. For example, on would use `\\[6pt]` to separate two rows of the table by 6 points of blank space.

A horizontal line in a table from column *i* to column *j* inclusive can be produced using \cline{*i*-*j*}. For example `\cline{3-5}` produces a horizontal line spanning columns 3, 4 and 5 of some table.

A control sequence of the form \multicolumn{*num*}{*fmt*}{*tex* can be used within the body of a table to produce an entry spanning several columns. Here *num* specifies the number of columns to be spanned, *fmt* specifies the format for the entry (e.g., `l` if the entry is to be left-justified, or `c` if it is to be centred), and *text* is the text of the entry. For example, to span three columns of a table with the words 'Year of Entry' (centred with respect to the three columns), one would use

```
\multicolumn{3}{c}{Year of entry}
```

3.13 Document Classes

As has already been discussed, all LaTeX documents must start with a document class declaration of the form

`\documentclass[`*options*`]{`*class*`}`

There are various classes to choose from; each alters the final output of the document in a particular way. To use a class, its name must be inserted between braces after the `\documentclass` command. There are several document classes:

- `article` for articles in scientific journals, presentations, short reports, computer documentation, & c.;
- `report` for longer reports containing several chapters, Ph.D. theses, and small books;
- `book` for real books;
- `slides` for overhead transparencies (this class uses big, sans serif lettering); and
- `proc` for event proceedings.

The documentclass command can take several optional arguments as well:

- 10pt, 11pt, 12pt set the size of the main font in the document; if no option is specified, 10pt is assumed.
- a4paper, a5paper, executivepaper, b5paper, legalpaper, and letterpaper set the paper size.
- fleqn typesets displayed formulæ left-aligned, rather than centred.
- leqno numbers formulæ on the left, rather than on the right.
- titlepage, notitlepage specifies whether to start a new page after the title or not. Unless otherwise specified, articles do not, but reports and books do.
- onecolumn, twocolumn typeset the document in one or two columns.
- openright, openany begin chapters on the right, or on the next available page. openright is default for books, and openany is default for reports. articles do not use chapters, so this option is not applicable.

3.14 Producing Letters

Although LATEX is most often associated with the production of doctoral theses in mathematics and physics, it can just as well be used to produce letters (of the *Dear John:* variety). The same hierarchical approach is used in writing a letter as in writing a book or report, but the names of the sectioning commands are different.

A LATEX-formatted letter begins with declaring the `letter` document class. In other words, the first line typed in is: `\documentclass{letter}`. Because the LATEX letter document style was originally made to produce a number of letters at once, the writer's name is signed, return address inserted, and letter(s) dated) at the *beginning* of the document. The preamble looks like so:

```
\documentclass{letter}
\signature{John Stephenson, 1st Earl of
           Blackacre, M.P., J.P., R.N.,
           M.B.Ch.B.}
\date{20 April 2012}
\address{420 Fleet-street, \\
         Suite 222B, \\
         Whitehall, S.W. 1, \\
```

```
            Gtr London, England}
\begin{document}
```

After this goes the text of the letter(s). Each letter is an environment; that is, each letter starts with the control sequence `\begin{letter}` and ends with the control sequence `\end{letter}`. The `letter` environment takes one, mandatory argument: the address of the recipient. After this, the opening is entered as the argument of the `\opening` control sequence, followed by the meat of the letter. Finally, the letter is closed using the `\closing` control sequence.

There are several control sequences which may be used after the `\closing`. Each of these takes one mandatory argument. `\ps` produces a *post scriptum*, `\cc` produces a list of carbon copy recipients, and `encl` produces an enclosures list.

For example, a typical letter might have,

```
\begin{letter}{Henry Thompson-Ellington,
               M.B.Ch.B., K.C.M.G., K.B.E. \\
               1 Harley-street, \\
               Unit 05, \\
               Westminster, S.W. 1, \\
               Gtr London, England}
```

```
\opening{Dear Lord Blackacre:}

Please send me any information you may have in
regards to indications, contra-indications,
dosing, addiction potential, discontinuation
symptoms, and overdosage management for the
drug {\it buprenorphine}.  I am most interested
in anecdotal information and off-label
indications, rather than what is published by
the press.

I am also giving a presentation at the Royal
Hospital, Chelsea, on differences in approach
when treating chemical dependency in the V.I.P.
or celebrity patient.  I eagerly await your
attendance.

Your prompt reply is appreciated.

\closing{Cordially,}
\ps{I truly enjoyed your discourse on pain
management in the p\ae diatric patient.  Well
done.  Thank you.}
```

```
\cc{John Watson, M.D.}
\encl{invitation}
\end{letter}
```

After the last letter comes the `\end{document}` statement.

3.15 Slides

LaTeX is not, nor does it want to be, PowerPoint. There are no animations available when making slides in LaTeX, and it is very hard to use five or six different fonts on one slide (this, perhaps, is intentional). There are situations, however, when this simplicity is actually a *good* thing, and these situations are probably more common than you think. Most specifically, this document class is best used when creating acetate transparencies for use in overhead projectors; the benefit of using LaTeX for this, rather than a word processor, is the facility by which mathematical formulæ may be included.

To make slides in LaTeX, use `\documentclass{slides}`. This is arguably the simplest of the various document classes available in LaTeX: there are no hierarchical commands, and the only environment particular to this document class is the `slides` environment, used for separating one slide from another.

The general form for a LATEX slides document is as follows:

```
\documentclass{slides}
\begin{slide}
slide one
\end{slide}
\begin{slide}
slide two
\end{slide}
\end{document}
```

There is no particular syntax for specifying the title of a slide; this is up to the author. Therefore, consistency is *crucial*. If the author has specified huge, italic text as the title of one slide, he should use huge, italic text on all the other slides. Instead of the usual font, LATEX will print text in large, sans-serif type.

Chapter 4

Further Features of LaTeX

4.1 Hyphenation

LaTeX hyphenates words wherever necessary. If the hyphenation algorithm does not find the correct hyphenation points, the situation can be remedied by means of the following control sequences to tell TeX about the exception.

The control sequence

```
\hyphenation{word-one word-two wordthree...}
```

causes the words listed in the argument to be hyphenated only at the points marked by a hyphen (-). The argument of the control sequence should only contain words built from letters (including accented letters).

The example below will allow 'hyphenation' to be hyphenated as well as 'Hyphenation', and it prevents 'FORTRAN', 'Fortran' and 'fortran' from being hyphenated at all.

```
\hyphenation{hy-phe-na-tion Fortran}
```

The control sequence `\-` inserts a 'discretionary' (user-specified) hyphen into a word. This becomes the only point hyphenation is allowed in this instance of this word; this control sequence is especially useful for words containing special characters (e.g. accented characters), because LaTeX does not automatically hyphenate words containing special characters unless permitted by the `\-` or `\hyphenation` control sequences. For instance, to allow the hyphenation of a particular instance of the word 'hôtel', use the control sequence `h\^{o}\-tel`.

Several words can be kept together on one line with the control sequence `\mbox{text}`. It causes its argument to be kept together under all circumstances, for example:

```
My phone number will change soon.  It will be
\mbox{0116 291 2319}.
```

4.2 User-Defined Control Sequences in LaTeX

Suppose that the document being worked on calls for the frequent use of a complex series of LaTeX commands. For example, suppose that attention is drawn to important passages with the aid of a thick black line on the outside margin of the page, like so:

> The following case is of some importance. Suppose that a_{rs} is a set of quantities whose tensor character is under investigation. Let X^r be an arbitrary contravarian vector. Suppose we are given that $a_{rs}X^r X^s$ is an invariant. What can we tell about the tensor character of a_{rs}?

This paragraph is obtained by typing

```
The following case is of some
importance.\marginpar{\rule[-10.5mm]{1mm}{10mm}}
Suppose that \(a_{rs}\) is a set of quantities
whose tensor character is under investigation.
Let \(X^r\) be an arbitrary contravarian
vector.  Suppose we are given that \(a_{rs}X^r
```

```
X^s\) is an invariant. What can we tell about
the tensor character of \(a_{rs}\)?
```

It would be nice if LaTeX allowed a shorter command to do this job, something like (perhaps) `\attn`. This can in fact be done, by defining a *macro* using `\newcommand`. In this case, a line with the control sequence

```
\newcommand{\attn}{\rule[-10.5mm]{1mm}{10mm}}
```

is placed in the preamble of the document (that is, between `\documentclass` and `\begin{document}`. Once that is done, creating the thick black line as above would only require typing `\attn`.

This procedure can be modified slightly to take variables, or *arguments*. For instance, suppose that an author wants technical words in his document <u>underscored</u> and definitions added as margin notes on the outside border. This is possible by hand-crafting a macro to take two arguments: the text to underscore, and the text to put in the margin note. The control sequence to put in the preamble would look like this:

his!

```
\newcommand{\gloss}[2]{\underline{#1}\marginpar{#2}}
```

and the new `\gloss` macro would be employed like this:

```
Here's a knocking indeed!  If a man were porter
of hell-gate, he should have \gloss{old}{Used
colloquially, perhaps in the sense 'plenty
of'.} turning the key.  Knock, knock, knock!
Who's there, in the name of Beelzebub?  Here's
a farmer that hanged himself on the
\gloss{expectation of plenty}{The farmer who
had been holding his grain off the market in
anticipation of high prices hanged himself when
prices dropped as the result of a promising
harvest.}; come in time; have
\gloss{napkins}{Handkerchiefs.} enough about
you; here you'll sweat for it.  Knock, knock!
Who's there, in the other devil's name?
```

What has happened is that the two phrases in curly brackets have replaced the variables #1 and #2 in the sequence of tags defined by `\newcommand`. The number 2 inside square brackets in the `\newcommand` line defining `\gloss` indicates to LaTeX that it is to expect two values inside curly brackets, replacing the two variables.

4.3 The pagestyle Command

By default, and depending on the class of the document under consideration, LaTeX supports three types of headers and footers. As a rule, articles generally use no header, but a footer consisting of the page number centred is printed. In contrast, reports and books use full headers and footers: the title of the current chapter or section is written as the header, and the page is (as with articles) centred in the footer. Finally, letters use no page numbering at all.

This can be changed using the `\pagestyle` command. This command is placed in the *preamble* (that is, between `\documentclass` and `\begin{document}`) and changes the header and footer for the *whole* document.

The `\pagestyle` command takes one of three possible arguments. `\pagestyle{plain}` puts the page number in the footer with nothing in the header; `\pagestyle{empty}` removes both the header and the footer; and `\pagestyle{headings}` will enable both header (with chapter names) and footer.

The type of header and footer can also be changed for the *current* page only, by using the `\thispagestyle` command instead. The syntax for `\thispagestyle` is the same as for `\pagestyle`, with the only exception being that it is placed in the *body* of the document.

Note that `\thispagestyle` only affects the *printing* of the relevant information; if one skipped, say, page six by means of the `\thispagestyle{empty}` command, the following page would be numbered seven.

4.4 Add-On Packages for LaTeX

4.4.1 Extra Line Spacing

In academia, instructors generally request additional space between lines, so that they may insert comments. LaTeX offers a facility for this (*viz.* the `\linespread` control sequence), but it is an all-or-nothing affair, and often tricky to use. For example, the control sequence `\linespread{1.3}` in the preamble of the document renders it effectively 'one-and-a-half spaced', while `\linespread{1.6}` sets up 'double spacing'.

Therefore, the add-on package `setspace` is used; it is included by typing the lines:

```
\usepackage{setspace}
\doublespacing
```

in the preamble of the document. This produces double spacing; in other words, there will be a line of white space equal in height to a line of text between every two lines of text. For one-and-a-half spacing, the second line can be replaced with the declaration `\onehalfspacing`. Technically speaking, one-and-a-half spacing refers to separating lines of text by white space equal in height to one-half of a line of text.

4.4.2 In-Paragraph Lists

In addition to bulleted and numbered lists, the requirement often arises for a list in line with the surrounding paragraph. One of the circumstances when in-paragraph, rather than numbered or bulleted, lists are preferred, is when condensing or paraphrasing a legal statute for easier reading. Unlike bulleted and numbered lists, in-paragraph lists are not supported natively by LaTeX; their construction, therefore, depends on the use of the add-on package `paralist`.

Inline lists generally use lowercase letters of the alphabet as counters, which are set off from the item text by a bracket; this can, however, be changed. The following document source:

```
\documentclass{article}
\usepackage{paralist}
\begin{document}
As of 1 July 2007 and per the Health Act 2006,
tobacco smoking is banned in certain workplaces
in England.  The Act, in effect, restricts
smoking in
\begin{inparaenum}[\itshape a\upshape )]
\item public places of work during business
hours and
\item places in which either more than one
person works or which offer services directly
to the public; but these restrictions apply
only to
\item the public part of a partially-public
workplace and
\item the enclosed part of a partially-enclosed
workplace.
\end{inparaenum}
\end{document}
```

would yield

As of 1 July 2007 and per the Health Act 2006, tobacco smoking is banned in certain workplaces in England. The Act, in effect, restricts smoking in *a*) public places of work during business hours and *b*) places in which either more than one person works or which offer services directly to the public; but these restrictions apply only to *c*) the public part of a partially-public workplace and *d*) the enclosed part of a partially-enclosed workplace.

`inparaenum` takes one optional argument: the form of the counter. This may in fact be anything, although the style tokens `A`, `a`, `I`, `i`, and `1` change the numbering system to capital and lowercase letters, capital and lowercase Roman numerals, and Arabic numerals respectively.

4.4.3 Chemistry

Inserting chemical diagrams in LaTeX is very complicated and beyond the scope of this book; typesetting chemical *equations*, however, is comparatively simple. They can be properly typeset in LaTeX using the package `mhchem`. The following example illustrates the use of the `mhchem` package:

```
\documentclass{article}
```

```
\usepackage[version=3]{mhchem}
\begin{document}
...
The terms ``strong'' and ``weak'' acid can be
explained by the Br\o nsted-Lowry concept and
also by comparing the reactions of acids with
the same base---for example, water.  Using
\ce{HA} as the general symbol for any acid and
\ce{A-} as its conjugate base, the empirically-%
derived table of acids and bases lists the
position of equilibrium of acids reacting with
water.

\centerline{\ce{HA_{(aq)} + H2O_{(l)} <=> A-_{(aq)}}
\end{document}
```

In the above document, <=> typesets the equilibrium arrows $\rightleftharpoons$. An unequal equilibrium that strongly favours the reactants uses <<=>, whereas one that strongly favours the products uses <=>>. Subscripts (in this case, of states of matter) are obtained with the underscore _. Otherwise, the chemical symbols are simply typed in after the control sequence \ce. The above source, when passed through LaTeX, yields

The terms "strong" and "weak" acid can be explained by the Brønsted-Lowry concept and also by comparing the reactions of acids with the same base—for example, water. Using HA as the general symbol for any acid and A^- as its conjugate base, the empirically-derived table of acids and bases lists the position of equilibrium of acids reacting with water.

$$HA_{(aq)} + H_2O_{(l)} \rightleftharpoons A-_{(aq)}$$

Precipitates and gases are typeset with v (the letter *vee*) and ^ respectively, set off from the chemical symbol with a space; the simple reactants $\longrightarrow$ product arrow is written as ->. For example, the document

```
A \textit{single replacement reaction} is
the reaction of an element with a compound
to produce a new element and an ionic
compound.  This reaction usually occurs in
aqu\ae ous solutions.  For example, silver
can be produced from copper and a solution
of silver ions:

\centerline{\ce{Cu + 2AgNO3 -> Cu(NO3)2 + Ag v}}
```

yields

A *single replacement reaction* is the reaction of an element with a compound to produce a new element and an ionic compound. This reaction usually offurs in aquæous solutions. For example, silver can be produced from copper and a solution of silver ions:

$$\mathrm{Cu} + 2\,\mathrm{AgNO_3} \longrightarrow \mathrm{Cu(NO_3)_2} + \mathrm{Ag}\downarrow$$

Single, double, and triple bonds use hyphens -, equal signs =, and hash signs #, respectively. For instance, the document

A *double bond* in *chemistry* is a chemical *bond* between two chemical *elements* involving four *bonding electrons* instead of the usual two. The most common double bond, that is between two carbon atoms, can be found in *alkenes*. Many types of double bonds exist between two different elements, such as in a *carbonyl* group with a carbon atom and an oxygen atom. Other common double bonds are found in *azo compounds* (N=N), *imines* (C=N) and *sulphoxides* (S=O). In skeletal formula the double bond is drawn as two parallel lines (=) between the two connected atoms; typographically, the equals sign is used for this.

A *triple bond*, in contrast, involves *six* bonding electrons. The most common triple bond, that between two *carbon atoms* (C≡C), can be found in *alkynes*. Other functional groups containing a triple bond are *cyanides* (C≡N) and *isocyanides* (N≡C). Some diatomic molecules, such as *dinitrogen* (N≡N) and *carbon monoxide* (C≡O) are also triply bonded. In skeletal formula the triple bond is drawn as three parallel lines between the two connected atoms; in typography, this is accomplished with the hash sign.

is produced by the source text

```
\textit{bonding electrons} instead of the
A \emph{double bond} in \textit{chemistry}
is a chemical \textit{bond} between two
chemical \textit{elements} involving
four \textit{bonding electrons} instead
of the usual two. The most common
double bond, that is between two carbon
atoms, can be found in \textit{alkenes}.
```

```
Many types of double bonds exist
between two different elements, such as
in a \emph{carbonyl} group with a
carbon atom and an oxygen atom. Other
common double bonds are found in \textit{azo
compounds} (\ce{N=N}), \textit{imines}
(\ce{C=N}) and \textit{sulphoxides}
(\ce{S=O}). In skeletal formula the
double bond is drawn as two parallel
lines (=) between the two connected
atoms; typographically, the equals sign
is used for this.

A \emph{triple bond}, in contrast,
involves \emph{six} bonding electrons.
The most common triple bond, that
between two \textit{carbon atoms}
(\ce{C#C}), can be found in
\textit{alkynes}. Other functional
groups containing a triple bond are
\textit{cyanides} (\ce{C#N}) and
\textit{isocyanides} (\ce{N#C}).  Some
diatomic molecules, such as
\textit{dinitrogen} (\ce{N#N}) and
```

```
\textit{carbon monoxide} (\ce{C#O}) are
also triply bonded. In skeletal formula
the triple bond is drawn as three
parallel lines between the two
connected atoms; in typography, this is
accomplished with the hash sign.
```

For example, the source text

```
Catalysts are substances that increase
the rate of a reaction, but are not
consumed in the process.  In some
cases, reactions occur at such a
glacial pace that, in the absence of a
catalyst, they are nearly useless.
Biological catalysts, known as enzymes,
are ubiquitous in living cells.

There are two important classes of
catalyst: \emph{homogenous} catalysts,
such as enzymes and aqu\ae ous ions,
are uniformly mixed with the reactants,
and \emph{heterogeneous} catalysts
provide a surface that holds and
```

```
reconfigures the reactants in order to
create a more favourable environment
for reaction to take place.

Homogeneous catalysts provide a faster
reaction path by facilitating the
formation of an unstable intermediate,
which quickly decomposes into end
products, for example:

\centerline{\ce{CH3CH2OH_{(g)} + HCl_{(g)}
->C[H2SO4] CH3CH2Cl + H2O}}

Ethanol and muriatic acid react in the
presence of vitriol to produce ethyl
chloride and water; the intermediate
product is \ce{CH3CH2OH2+}, which is
unstable, and quickly reacts with
\ce{Cl-} to produce the products.

Another example is the biologically-%
catalysed conversion of hydrogen
peroxide to water and oxygen in the
presence of the catalase enzyme.  The
```

```
notation for this is:

\centerline{\ce{H2O2 ->T[catalase] H2O
+ O2_{(g)}}}
```

yields

Catalysts are substances that increase the rate of a reaction, but are not consumed in the process. In some cases, reactions occur at such a glacial pace that, in the absence of a catalyst, they are nearly useless. Biological catalysts, known as enzymes, are ubiquitous in living cells.

There are two important classes of catalyst: *homogenous* catalysts, such as enzymes and aquæous ions, are uniformly mixed with the reactants, and *heterogeneous* catalysts provide a surface that holds and reconfigures the reactants in order to create a more favourable environment for reaction to take place.

Homogeneous catalysts provide a faster reaction path by facilitating the formation of an unstable intermediate, which quickly decomposes into end products, for example:

$$CH_3CH_2OH_{(g)} + HCl_{(g)} \xrightarrow{H_2SO_4} CH_3CH_2Cl + H_2O$$

Ethanol and muriatic acid react in the presence of vitriol to produce ethyl chloride and water; the intermediate product is $CH_3CH_2OH_2{}^+$, which is unstable, and quickly reacts with Cl^- to produce the products.

Another example is the biologically-catalysed conversion of hydrogen peroxide to water and oxygen in the presence of the catalase enzyme. The notation for this is:

$$H_2O_2 \xrightarrow{\text{catalase}} H_2O + O_{2(g)}$$

4.4.4 Line-Wrapped Tables

The `tabular` environment in LaTeX has one large flaw: it is exceedingly difficult to make a table whose text 'wraps' across lines. If the text to include in a cell of a table is too long, it will simply continue off the page, necessitating that it be manually split into two or more rows. This is unacceptable. Thankfully, there are two solutions. If the exact width of the text is known, it can be manually specified, as in this example using the traditional `tabular` environment for typesetting tables.

```
\begin{tabular}{ | l | l | l | p{7cm} |}
\hline
Day & Hi & Lo & Summary \\ \hline
Mon & 11 & 22 & A clear day with lots
                of sunshine.  However,
                the strong breeze will
                bring down the tempera%
                tures.\\ \hline
Tue & 9 & 19 & Cloudy with rain, across
               many northern regions.
               Clear spells across
               most of Scotland and
               Northern Ireland, but
               rain reaching the far
               northwest. \\ \hline
Wed & 10 & 21 & Rain will still linger
                for the morning.  Con%
                ditions will improve by
                early afternoon and
                continue throughout
                the evening. \\
                     \hline
\end{tabular}
```

produces

Day	Hi	Lo	Summary
Mon	11	22	A clear day with lots of sunshine. However, the strong breeze will bring down the temperatures.
Tue	9	19	Cloudy with rain, across many northern regions. Clear spells across most of Scotland and Northern Ireland, but rain reaching the far northwest.
Wed	10	21	Rain will still linger for the morning. Conditions will improve by early afternoon and continue throughout the evening.

It does look presentable, but creating it takes a certain amount of intuitive knowledge on how LATEX measures pages, as well as the liberal application of what was, in decades past, referred to as 'elbow grease'. Again, given the modern state of the world, this is unacceptable; it is perhaps easier in the above case to use a word processor and have done with it—although that is more easily said than done.

For instance, the original table had the names of the weekdays spelled out in full; this, however, wasted so much space that, even with wrapping enabled, the table still would not fit on a sheet of DIN A5 paper. The length of the column was shortened, but this resulted in an altogether different sort of ugliness.

The `tabu` extension goes a long way towards remedying this problem; it automatically measures, and adapts to, the line width. The syntax is only very slightly different to that of `tabular`. The obvious difference is that when using `tabu` to typeset tables, the line `\usepackage{tabu}` must be put in the document's preamble. Another difference is that instead of LaTeX calculating the width of the table automatically, it calculates it in terms of `\textwidth`. For example, LaTeX can be instructed to make a table precisely 80% of the text width. Finally, there is one more possible column designator in addition to the usual `l`, `c`, `r`, and `p`; this argument, `X`, is what makes `tabu` distinctive.

`X` means that the column in question is *expandable*. The technical mechanics of this are that `X` columns are typeset last of all: after LaTeX typesets all the *fixed* columns to have no more width than there *needs* to be, LaTeX typesets the expandable columns to take up the *remainder* of the width. `X` takes one argument: the number of 'columns' to span. For instance, if a table has a column designated `X` and another designated `X[2]`, the second column will be twice the width of the first.

This seems obtuse, but it really is not. Here is an example of its use:

```
\begin{tabu} to \linewidth {|l|X|}
\hline
{\bf Area} & {\bf Forecast}
Viking & Cyclonic becoming
         north 5 to 7,
         occasionally gale 8.
         Rough or very rough,
         occasionally high.
         Rain or wintry
         showers.  Good,
         occasionally poor.
         \\ \hline
N.\ Utsire, S.\ Utsire
       & Southeasterly
         backing northerly
         later, 5 to 7,
         occasionally gale
         8.  Rough or very
         rough.  Wintry
         showers.  Good,
```

```
            occasionally poor.
            \\ \hline
  Forties & In east, cyclonic
             5 or 6, becoming
             northerly 6 or 7,
             perhaps gale 8
             later. In west,
             northerly or
             northwesterly 7
             to severe gale 9.
             In east, rough or
             very rough. in
             west, rough or
             very rough,
             occasionally high.
             In east, wintry
             showers. In west,
             squally wintry
             showers.  Good,
             occasionally poor.
             \\ \hline
\end{tabu}
```

This produces a much nicer table:

Area	**Forecast**
Viking	Cyclonic becoming north 5 to 7, occasionally gale 8. Rough or very rough, occasionally high. Rain or wintry showers. Good, occasionally poor.
N. Utsire, S. Utsire	Southeasterly backing northerly later, 5 to 7, occasionally gale 8. Rough or very rough. Wintry showers. Good, occasionally poor.
Forties	In east, cyclonic 5 or 6, becoming northerly 6 or 7, perhaps gale 8 later. In west, northerly or northwesterly 7 to severe gale 9. In east, rough or very rough. in west, rough or very rough, occasionally high. In east, wintry showers. In west, squally wintry showers. Good, occasionally poor.

4.4.5 Colours in LaTeX

In some cases, especially when the document is to be predominantly displayed on the screen, the use of colour is necessary. This can be done with the `color` package, by inserting the control sequence `\usepackage{color}` (note the American spelling!) in the preamble of the document. This permits the use of eight colours:

Red	Red
Green	
Blue	Blue
Cyan	Cyan
Magenta	Magenta
Yellow	
Black	Black

More colours might be obtained by using the control sequence

```
\usepackage[usenames,dvipsnames,svgnames]{color}
```

This allows the use of a staggering one hundred and eighty different colours, in addition to those listed above. To wit, these are:

`AliceBlue`	
`AntiqueWhite`	
`Apricot`	Apricot
`Aqua`	
`Aquamarine`	
`Azure`	
`Beige`	
`Bisque`	
`Bittersweet`	Bittersweet
`BlanchedAlmond`	
`BlueGreen`	BlueGreen
`BlueViolet`	BlueViolet
`BrickRed`	BrickRed
`Brown`	Brown
`BurlyWood`	BurlyWood
`BurntOrange`	BurntOrange
`CadetBlue`	CadetBlue
`CarnationPink`	CarnationPink
`Cerulean`	Cerulean
`Chartreuse`	
`Chocolate`	Chocolate
`Coral`	Coral
`CornflowerBlue`	CornflowerBlue
`Cornsilk`	

`Crimson`	Crimson
`Dandelion`	Dandelion
`DarkBlue`	DarkBlue
`DarkCyan`	DarkCyan
`DarkGoldenrod`	DarkGoldenrod
`DarkGreen`	DarkGreen
`DarkGrey`	DarkGrey
`DarkKhaki`	DarkKhaki
`DarkMagenta`	DarkMagenta
`DarkOliveGreen`	DarkOliveGreen
`DarkOrange`	DarkOrange
`DarkOrchid`	DarkOrchid
`DarkRed`	DarkRed
`DarkSalmon`	DarkSalmon
`DarkSeaGreen`	DarkSeaGreen
`DarkSlateBlue`	DarkSlateBlue
`DarkSlateGrey`	DarkSlateGrey
`DarkTurquoise`	DarkTurquoise
`DarkViolet`	DarkViolet
`DeepPink`	DeepPink
`DeepSkyBlue`	DeepSkyBlue
`DimGrey`	DimGrey
`DodgerBlue`	DodgerBlue
`Emerald`	Emerald

`FireBrick`	FireBrick
`FloralWhite`	
`ForestGreen`	ForestGreen
`Fuchsia`	Fuchsia
`Gainsboro`	
`GhostWhite`	
`Gold`	
`Goldenrod`	Goldenrod
`Green`	Green
`GreenYellow`	
`Grey`	Grey
`Honeydew`	
`HotPink`	HotPink
`IndianRed`	IndianRed
`Indigo`	Indigo
`Ivory`	
`JungleGreen`	JungleGreen
`Khaki`	
`Lavender`	
`LavenderBlush`	
`LawnGreen`	
`LemonChiffon`	
`LightBlue`	LightBlue
`LightCoral`	LightCoral

`LightCyan`	
`LightGoldenrodYellow`	
`LightGreen`	LightGreen
`LightGrey`	LightGrey
`LightPink`	LightPink
`LightSalmon`	LightSalmon
`LightSeaGreen`	LightSeaGreen
`LightSkyBlue`	LightSkyBlue
`LightSlateGrey`	LightSlateGrey
`LightSteelBlue`	LightSteelBlue
`LightYellow`	
`Lime`	Lime
`LimeGreen`	LimeGreen
`Linen`	
`Mahogany`	Mahogany
`Maroon`	Maroon
`MediumAquamarine`	MediumAquamarine
`MediumBlue`	MediumBlue
`MediumOrchid`	MediumOrchid
`MediumPurple`	MediumPurple
`MediumSeaGreen`	MediumSeaGreen
`MediumSlateBlue`	MediumSlateBlue
`MediumSpringGreen`	MediumSpringGreen
`MediumTurquoise`	MediumTurquoise

`MediumVioletRed`	MediumVioletRed
`Melon`	Melon
`MidnightBlue`	MidnightBlue
`MintCream`	
`MistyRose`	
`Moccasin`	
`Mulberry`	Mulberry
`NavajoWhite`	
`Navy`	Navy
`NavyBlue`	NavyBlue
`Olive`	Olive
`OldLace`	
`OliveDrab`	OliveDrab
`OliveGreen`	OliveGreen
`Orange`	Orange
`OrangeRed`	OrangeRed
`Orchid`	Orchid
`PaleGoldenrod`	
`PaleGreen`	
`PaleTurquoise`	
`PaleVioletRed`	PaleVioletRed
`PapayaWhip`	
`Peach`	Peach
`PeachPuff`	

`Periwinkle` Periwinkle
`Peru` Peru
`PineGreen` PineGreen
`Pink` Pink
`Plum` Plum
`PowderBlue` PowderBlue
`ProcessBlue` ProcessBlue
`Purple` Purple
`RawSienna` RawSienna
`RedOrange` RedOrange
`RedViolet` RedViolet
`Rhodamine` Rhodamine
`RosyBrown` RosyBrown
`RoyalBlue` RoyalBlue
`RoyalPurple` RoyalPurple
`RubineRed` RubineRed
`SaddleBrown` SaddleBrown
`Salmon` Salmon
`SandyBrown` SandyBrown
`SeaGreen` SeaGreen
`Seashell`
`Sepia` Sepia
`Sienna` Sienna
`Silver` Silver

`SkyBlue`	SkyBlue
`SlateBlue`	SlateBlue
`SlateGrey`	SlateGrey
`Snow`	
`SpringGreen`	SpringGreen
`SteelBlue`	SteelBlue
`Tan`	Tan
`Teal`	Teal
`TealBlue`	TealBlue
`Thistle`	Thistle
`Tomato`	Tomato
`Turquoise`	Turquoise
`Violet`	Violet
`VioletRed`	VioletRed
`Wheat`	Wheat
`White`	
`WhiteSmoke`	
`WildStrawberry`	WildStrawberry
`YellowGreen`	YellowGreen
`YellowOrange`	YellowOrange

The control sequence `\color{`*name*`}` (again, note the American spelling!) is used to change the colour of text. It is used in the manner of a declaration; that is, the colour change takes effect from the point that the command is issued until the end of the current group. For example:

> The first versions of Mosaic and Netscape Navigator used the X11 colour names as the basis for their colour lists, as both started as X Window System applications. Web colours have an unambiguous colorimetric definition, sRGB, which relates the chromaticities of a particular phosphor set, a given transfer curve, adaptive whitepoint, and viewing conditions. These have been chosen to be similar to many real-world monitors and viewing conditions, so that, even without colour management, rendering is fairly close to the specified values. However, user agents vary in the fidelity with which they represent the specified colours. More advanced user agents use colour management to provide better colour fidelity; this is particularly important for Web-to-print applications.

is produced with the source:

```
The first versions of {\color{ProcessBlue}
Mosaic} and {\color{ProcessBlue} Netscape
```

Navigator} used the {\color{ProcessBlue} X11 colour names} as the basis for their {\color{ProcessBlue} colour lists}, as both started as {\color{ProcessBlue} X Window System} applications. {\color{ProcessBlue} Web colours} have an unambiguous colorimetric definition, {\color{ProcessBlue} sRGB}, which relates the {\color{ProcessBlue}chromaticicities} of a particular {\color{ProcessBlue} phosphor} set, a given transfer curve, adaptive whitepoint, and viewing conditions. These have been chosen to be similar to many real-world {\color{ProcessBlue} monitors} and viewing conditions, so that, even without {\color{ProcessBlue} colour management}, rendering is fairly close to the specified values. However, {\color{ProcessBlue} user agents} vary in the fidelity with which they represent the specified colours. More advanced user agents use colour management to provide better colour fidelity; this is particularly important for {\color{ProcessBlue} Web-to-print} applications.

It is also possible to change the *background* of text. This can be done with the control sequence

`\colorbox{`*declared-colour*`}{`*text*`}`

Note, again, the American spelling, and also note that this control sequence *prevents hyphenation*. For instance, the following text:

> Nigel Paul Farage (born 3 April 1964) is a British politician and leader of the UK Independence Party since 2010, a position he also held from September 2006 to November 2009. Since 1999, he has been an MEP for South East England. He co-chairs the Europe of Freedom and Direct Democracy group. Farage was a founding member of UKIP, having left the Conservative Party in 1992 after the signing of the Maastricht Treaty. Having unsuccessfully campaigned in European and Westminster parliamentary elections for UKIP since 1994, he won a seat as MEP for South East England in the 1999 European Parliamentary Election—the first year the regional list system was used—and was re-elected in 2004, 2009, and 2014.

may be produced by the code:

```
\colorbox{black}{\color{white} Nigel Paul
Farage} (born 3 April 1964) is a
\colorbox{black}{\color{white}British}
politician and leader of the UK Independence
Party since 2010, a position he also held from
September 2006 to November 2009. Since 1999, he
has been an \colorbox{black}{\color{white}MEP}
for South East England. He co-chairs the Europe
of Freedom and Direct Democracy group.
Farage was a founding member of UKIP,
having left the \colorbox{black}{\color{white}
Conservative} Party in 1992 after the signing
of the \colorbox{black}{\color{white}
Maastricht} Treaty. Having unsuccessfully
campaigned in European and Westminster
parliamentary elections for UKIP since 1994, he
won a \colorbox{black}{\color{white} seat} as
MEP for \colorbox{black}{\color{white} South
East England} in the
\colorbox{black}{\color{white} 1999} European
Parliamentary Election---the first year the
regional list system was used---and was
```

```
re-elected in 2004,
2009, and 2014.
```

Chapter 5

Producing Mathematical Formulæ using LaTeX

5.1 Mathematics Mode

In order to obtain a mathematical formula using LaTeX, one must enter *mathematics mode* before the formula and leave it afterwards. Mathematical formulæ can occur either embedded in text or else displayed between lines of text. When a formula occurs within the text of a paragraph, the control sequence \(should be used to enter mathematics mode and the control sequence \) to leave it. For example, the text

> Let f be the function defined by $f(x) = 3x + 7$, and let a be a positive real number.

is produced by typing:

```
Let \(f\) be the function defined by
\(f(x) = 3x + 7\), and let \(a\) be
a positive real number.
```

In particular, note that even mathematical expressions consisting of a single character, like f and a in the example above, are placed within \(...\). This is not only to ensure that they are set in italic type, as is customary in mathematical typesetting, but also to establish the semantic *meaning* of the specified text: that is, that the character is used in its *mathematical* context.

LaTeX also allows the use of the dollar sign ($) to enter and leave mathematics mode. This is a throwback to the earlier Plain TeX markup language; \(\) does not work in Plain TeX. Thus,

> Let f be the function defined by $f(x) = 3x + 7$.

may be produced by typing

```
Let \( f \) be the function defined by
\( f(x) = 3x + 7 \).
```

The control sequences `\[` and `\]` are used to display a mathematical formula or equation on a line by itself. The output

If $f(x) = 3x + 7$ and $g(x) = x + 4$ then

$$f(x) + g(x) = 4x + 11$$

and

$$f(x)g(x) = 3x^2 + 19x + 28$$

may be produced by typing

```
If \(f(x) = 3x + 7\)
and \(g(x) = x + 4\) then
\[ f(x) + g(x) = 4x + 11\]
and
\[f(x)g(x) = 3x^2 + 19x +28\]
```

The Plain TeX syntax for displayed equations is $$...$$. Old-school syntax can still be used, like so:

If $f(x) = 3x + 7$ and $g(x) = x + 4$ then

$$f(x) + g(x) = 4x + 11$$

and

$$f(x)g(x) = 3x^2 + 19x + 28$$

This will produce:

```
If $f(x) = 3x + 7$
and $g(x) = x + 4$ then
$$ f(x) + g(x) = 4x + 11$$
and
$$f(x)g(x) = 3x^2 + 19x +28$$
```

There are a few downsides to this, though. First of all, they are inherited from a far older typesetting system and, in certain rare cases, do not quite work as intended. Second, the opening command is the same as the closing command. This can turn out to be quite confusing. That said, the `$...$` and `$$...$$` is a valid stylistic choice and does not need to be discouraged.

LaTeX provides facilities for the automatic numbering of displayed equations. Numbered equations may be produced by means of the control sequences `\begin{equation}` and `\end{equation}`. Thus

```
If \(f(x) = 3x + 7\)
and \(g(x) = x + 4\) then
\begin{equation}
f(x) + g(x) = 4x + 11
\end{equation}
and
\begin{equation}
f(x)g(x) = 3x^2 + 19x +28.
\end{equation}
```

produces

If $f(x) = 3x + 7$ and $g(x) = x + 4$ then

$$f(x) + g(x) = 4x + 11 \tag{5.1}$$

and

$$f(x)g(x) = 3x^2 + 19x + 28. \tag{5.2}$$

5.2 Characters in Mathematics Mode

All the characters on the keyboard have their standard meaning in mathematics mode, with the exception of the characters

```
# $ % & ~ _ ^ \ { } '
```

Normally, letters are set in italic type (unless the document uses a package called Concrete, in which italics are replaced by a distinctive font known as Euler). In mathematics mode the character ' has a special meaning: typing `\(u' + v''\)` produces $u' + v''$.

When LaTeX is in mathematics mode, any spaces between letters and other symbols in the source document do not affect the spacing of the final result, since LaTeX determines the spacing of characters in formulæ by its own internal rules. Both `\(u v + w = x\)` and `\(uv+w=x\)` therefore produce $uv + w = x$

Carriage returns may also be entered where necessary in your input file (e.g., in a complex formula with many Greek characters and technical symbols) and this will also have no effect on the final result, whether in text or maths mode.

The characters

```
#   $   %   &   _   {   }
```

are produced in mathematics mode by typing

```
\#   \$   \%   \&   \_   \{   \} .
```

To obtain \ in mathematics mode, the control sequence `\backslash` may be used.

5.3 Superscripts & Subscripts

Subscripts and superscripts are obtained using the special characters _ and ^ respectively. For example, the identity

$$ds^2 = dx_1^2 + dx_2^2 + dx_3^2 - c^2 dt^2$$

is obtained by typing

```
\[ ds^2 = dx_1^2 + dx_2^2 + dx_3^2 - c^2 dt^2 \]
```

It can also be obtained by typing

```
\[ ds^2 = dx^2_1 + dx^2_2 + dx^2_3 - c^2 dt^2 \]
```

since, when a superscript is to appear above a subscript, it is immaterial whether the superscript or subscript is the first to be specified.

Where more than one character occurs in a superscript or subscript, the characters involved should be enclosed in curly brackets. For example, the polynomial $x^{17} - 1$ is obtained by typing `\(x^{17} - 1\)`.

Expressions such as `\(s^n^j\)` are ambiguous and could be interpreted either as s^{nj} or as s^{n^j}. LaTeX therefore 'helpfully' (many exasperated mathematics authors would disagree) solicits attention by typing out an error. The first of these alternatives is obtained by typing `\(s^{n j}\)`, the second by typing `\(s^{n^j}\)`. A similar remark applies to subscripts. Note that the preceding example also demonstrates the use of double superscripts (where a superscript is placed on a superscript) and double subscripts.

It is sometimes necessary to obtain expressions in which the horizontal ordering of the subscripts is significant. The null group {} may be used to separate superscripts and subscripts that must follow one another. For example, the identity

$$R_i{}^j{}_{kl} = g^{jm} R_{imkl} = - g^{jm} R_{mikl} = - R^j{}_{ikl}$$

can be obtained by typing

```
\[ R_i{}^j{}_{kl} = g^{jm} R_{imkl}
   = - g^{jm} R_{mikl} = - R^j{}_{ikl} \]
```

5.4 Greek Letters

Lower case Greek letters are produced in mathematics mode by preceding the name of the letter by a backslash `\`. For example, the input `\(A = \pi r^2\)` produces the formula $A = \pi r^2$.

Here are the control sequences for the standard forms of the lowercase Greek letters:-

α	`\alpha`	ι	`\iota`	ρ	`\rho`
β	`\beta`	κ	`\kappa`	σ	`\sigma`
γ	`\gamma`	λ	`\lambda`	τ	`\tau`
δ	`\delta`	μ	`\mu`	υ	`\upsilon`
ϵ	`\epsilon`	ν	`\nu`	ϕ	`\phi`
ζ	`\zeta`	ξ	`\xi`	χ	`\chi`
η	`\eta`	o	`o`	ψ	`\psi`
θ	`\theta`	π	`\pi`	ω	`\omega`

Because omicron has precisely the same shape as the Latin letter o, there is no control sequence for it: simply type o.

Some Greek letters occur in variant forms. The variant forms are obtained by preceding the name of the Greek letter by 'var'. The following table lists the usual form of these letters and the variant forms:-

ϵ	\epsilon	ε	\varepsilon
θ	\theta	ϑ	\vartheta
π	\pi	ϖ	\varpi
ρ	\rho	ϱ	\varrho
σ	\sigma	ς	\varsigma
ϕ	\phi	φ	\varphi

Upper case Greek letters are obtained by making the first character of the name upper case; many of the upper case Greek letters look like upper case Latin letters, in which case they are entered as Latin letters. Here are the control sequences for the uppercase letters:

Γ	\Gamma	Ξ	\Xi	Φ	\Phi
Δ	\Delta	Π	\Pi	Ψ	\Psi
Θ	\Theta	Σ	\Sigma	Ω	\Omega
Λ	\Lambda	Υ	\Upsilon		

5.5 Mathematical Symbols

There are numerous mathematical symbols that can be used in mathematics mode. These are obtained by typing the appropriate control sequence.

"Large" Operators:

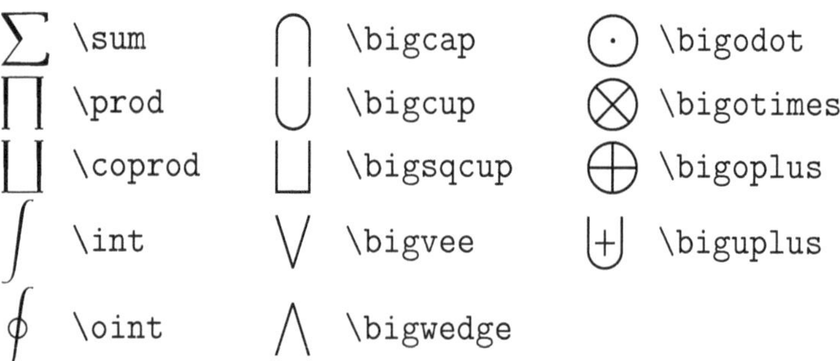

Binary Operations:

$\pm$	\pm	$\cap$	\cap	$\vee$	\vee
$\mp$	\mp	$\cup$	\cup	$\wedge$	\wedge
$\setminus$	\setminus	$\uplus$	\uplus	$\oplus$	\oplus
$\cdot$	\cdot	$\sqcap$	\sqcap	$\ominus$	\ominus
$\times$	\times	$\sqcup$	\sqcup	$\otimes$	\otimes
$\ast$	\ast		\triangleleftŕ		
$\star$	\star	$\triangleright$	\triangleright	$\odot$	\odot
$\diamond$	\diamond	$\wr$	\wr	$\dagger$	\dagger
$\circ$	\circ	$\bigcirc$	\bigcirc	$\ddagger$	\ddagger
$\bullet$	\bullet	$\bigtriangleup$	\bigtriangleup	$\amalg$	\amalg
$\div$	\div	$\bigtriangledown$	\bigtriangledown		

Relations:

$\leq$	`\leq`	$\geq$	`\geq`	$\equiv$	`\equiv`
$\prec$	`\prec`	$\succ$	`\succ`	$\sim$	`\sim`
$\preceq$	`\preceq`	$\succeq$	`\succeq`	$\simeq$	`\simeq`
$\ll$	`\ll`	$\gg$	`\gg`	$\asymp$	`\asymp`
$\subset$	`\subset`	$\supset$	`\supset`	$\approx$	`\approx`
$\subseteq$	`\subseteq`	$\supseteq$	`\supseteq`	$\cong$	`\cong`
$\sqsubseteq$	`\sqsubseteq`	$\sqsupseteq$	`\sqsupseteq`	$\bowtie$	`\bowtie`
$\in$	`\in`	$\ni$	`\ni`	$\propto$	`\propto`
$\vdash$	`\vdash`	$\dashv$	`\dashv`	$\models$	`\models`
$\smile$	`\smile`	$\mid$	`\mid`	$\doteq$	`\doteq`
$\frown$	`\frown`	$\parallel$	`\parallel`	$\perp$	`\perp`

Negated Relations:

$\not<$	`\not<`	$\not>$	`\not>`	$\neq$	`\no`
$\not\leq$	`\not\leq`	$\not\geq$	`\not\geq`	$\not\equiv$	`\no`
$\not\prec$	`\not\prec`	$\not\succ$	`\not\succ`	$\not\sim$	`\no`
$\not\preceq$	`\not\preceq`	$\not\succeq$	`\not\succeq`	$\not\simeq$	`\no`
$\not\subset$	`\not\subset`	$\not\supset$	`\not\supset`	$\not\approx$	`\no`
$\not\subseteq$	`\not\subseteq`	$\not\supseteq$	`\not\supseteq`	$\not\cong$	`\no`
$\not\sqsubseteq$	`\not\sqsubseteq`	$\not\sqsupseteq$	`\not\sqsupseteq`	$\not\asymp$	`\no`

Arrows:

$\leftarrow$	\leftarrow	$\rightarrow$	\rightarrow
$\longleftarrow$	\longleftarrow	$\longrightarrow$	\longrightarrow
$\Leftarrow$	\Leftarrow	$\Rightarrow$	\Rightarrow
$\Longleftarrow$	\Longleftarrow	$\Longrightarrow$	\Longrightarrow
$\leftrightarrow$	\leftrightarrow	$\Leftrightarrow$	\Leftrightarrow
$\longleftrightarrow$	\longleftrightarrow	$\Longleftrightarrow$	\Longleftrightarrow
$\hookleftarrow$	\hookleftarrow	$\hookrightarrow$	\hookrightarrow
$\leftharpoonup$	\leftharpoonup	$\rightharpoonup$	\rightharpoonup
$\leftharpoondown$	\leftharpoondown	$\rightharpoondown$	\rightharpoondown
$\uparrow$	\uparrow	$\downarrow$	\downarrow
$\Uparrow$	\Uparrow	$\Downarrow$	\Downarrow
$\updownarrow$	\updownarrow	$\Updownarrow$	\Updownarrow
$\nearrow$	\nearrow	$\nwarrow$	\nwarrow
$\searrow$	\searrow	$\swarrow$	\swarrow
$\mapsto$	\mapsto	$\longmapsto$	\longmapsto
$\rightleftharpoons$	\rightleftharpoons		

Openings:

$[$	\lbrack	$\lfloor$	\lfloor	$\lceil$	\lceil
$\{$	\lbrace	$\langle$	\langle		

Closings:

$]$	\rbrack	$\rfloor$	\rfloor	$\rceil$	\rceil
$\}$	\rbrace	$\rangle$	\rangle		

Miscellaneous Symbols:

$\aleph$	\aleph	$\prime$	\prime	$\forall$	\forall
$\hbar$	\hbar	$\emptyset$	\emptyset	$\exists$	\exists
$\imath$	\imath	∇	\nabla	$\neg$	\neg
$\jmath$	\jmath	$\surd$	\surd	$\flat$	\flat
ℓ	\ell	$\top$	\top	$\natural$	\natural
$\wp$	\wp	$\bot$	\bot	$\sharp$	\sharp
$\Re$	\Re	$\|$	\\|	$\clubsuit$	\clubsuit
$\Im$	\Im	$\angle$	\angle	$\diamondsuit$	\diamondsuit
∂	\partial	$\triangle$	\triangle	$\heartsuit$	\heartsuit
∞	\infty	$\backslash$	\backslash	$\spadesuit$	\spadesuit

Alternative Names:

$\neq$	\ne or \neq?=	
$\leq$	\le	(same as \leq)
$\geq$	\ge	(same as \geq)
$\{$	\{	(same as \lbrace)
$\}$	\}	(same as \lbrace)
$\to$	\to	(same as \rightarrow)
$\gets$	\gets	(same as \leftarrow)
$\owns$	\owns	(same as \ni)
$\land$	\land	(same as \wedge)
$\lor$	\lor	(same as \vee)
$\lnot$	\lnot	(same as \neg)
$\vert$	\vert	(same as |)
$\Vert$	\Vert	(same as \\|)
$\iff$	\iff	(same as \Longleftrightarrow, b extra space at each end)
$\colon$	\colon	(same as :, but with less space ar less likelihood of a line break af

5.6 Changing Fonts in Mathematics Mode

The 'math italic' font is automatically used in mathematics mode unless explicit instructions to the contrary are issued.

The rules for changing the font in mathematics mode are rather different to those applying when typesetting ordinary text. In mathematics mode, any change only applies to the single character or symbol that follows (or to any text enclosed within curly brackets immediately following the control sequence). Also, to change a character to the roman or boldface font, the control sequences `\mathrm` and `\mathbf` must be used (rather than `\textrm` and `\textbf`).

The following example illustrates the use of boldface in mathematical formulæ . The output

> Let $\mathbf{u}$, $\mathbf{v}$ and $\mathbf{w}$ be three vectors in ${\mathbf R}^3$. The volume V of the parallelepiped with corners at the points $\mathbf{0}$, $\mathbf{u}$, $\mathbf{v}$, $\mathbf{w}$, $\mathbf{u}+\mathbf{v}$, $\mathbf{u}+\mathbf{w}$, $\mathbf{v}+\mathbf{w}$ and $\mathbf{u}+\mathbf{v}+\mathbf{w}$ is given by the formula
>
> $$V = (\mathbf{u} \times \mathbf{v}) \cdot \mathbf{w}.$$

is produced by typing

```
Let \(\mathbf{u}\), \(\mathbf{v}\) and
\(\mathbf{w}\) be three vectors in
\({\mathbf R}^3\). The volume~\(V\) of
the parallelepiped with corners at the
points \(\mathbf{0}\), \(\mathbf{u}\),
```

```
\(\mathbf{v}\), \(\mathbf{w}\),
\(\mathbf{u}+\mathbf{v}\),
\(\mathbf{u}+\mathbf{w}\),
\(\mathbf{v}+\mathbf{w}\) and
\(\mathbf{u}+\mathbf{v}+\mathbf{w}\) is
given by the formula \[ V = (\mathbf{u}
\times \mathbf{v}) \cdot \mathbf{w}.\]
```

There is also a 'calligraphic' font available in mathematics mode. This is obtained using the control sequence `\cal`. *This font can only be used for uppercase letters.* These calligraphic letters have the form

$$\mathcal{ABCDEFGHIJKLMNOPQRSTUVWXYZ}.$$

5.7 Standard Functions (sin, cos etc.)

The names of certain standard functions and abbreviations are obtained by typing a backlash \ before the name. For example, one obtains

$$\cos(\theta + \phi) = \cos\theta\cos\phi - \sin\theta\sin\phi$$

by typing

```
\[ \cos(\theta + \phi) = \cos \theta
\cos \phi - \sin \theta \sin \phi \]
```

The following standard functions are represented by control sequences defined in LaTeX:

\arccos	\cos	\csc	\exp	\ker	\limsup	\min	\sinh
\arcsin	\cosh?	\gcd	\lg	\ln	\Pr	\sup	
\arctan	\cot	\det	\hom	\lim	\log	\sec	\tan
\arg	\coth	\dim	\inf	\liminf	\max	\sin	\tanh

Names of functions and other abbreviations not in this list can be obtained by converting to the roman font. Thus one obtains $\mathrm{cosec} A$ by typing `\(\mathrm{cosec} A\)`. Note that if one were to type simply `\(cosec A\)` one would obtain $cosec A$, because LaTeX has treated `cosec A` as the product of six quantities c, o, s, e, c and A and typeset the formula accordingly.

5.8 Text Embedded in Displayed Equations

Text can be embedded in displayed equations by using `\mbox{`*emb- text*`}`. For example, the formula

$$M^\perp = \{f \in V' : f(m) = 0 \mbox{ for all } m \in M\}.$$

is produced by typing

```
\[ M^\bot=\{ f \in V' : f(m) = 0
\mbox{ for all } m \in M \}.\]
```

Note the blank spaces before and after the words 'for all' in the above example. Had the input been

```
\[ M^\bot=\{ f \in V' : f(m)=0
\mbox{for all} m \in M \}.\]
```

the output would instead have been

$$M^\perp = \{f \in V' : f(m) = 0\mbox{for all}m \in M\}.$$

(In Plain TEX one should use `\hbox` in place of `\mbox`.)

5.9 Fractions and Roots

Vulgar fractions are obtained in LATEX using the construction `\frac{`*numerator*`}{`*denominator*`}`. For example:

The function f is given by

$$f(x) = 2x + \frac{x - 7}{x^2 + 4}$$

for all real numbers x.

is produced by typing

```
The function \(f\) is given by \[ f(x)
= 2x + \frac{x - 7}{x^2 + 4}\] for all
real numbers \(x\).
```

The control sequence `\sqrt{`*expression*`}` produces square roots. For example:

The roots of a quadratic polynomial ax^2+bx+c with $a \neq 0$ are given by the formula

$$\frac{-b \pm \sqrt{b^2 - 4ac}}{2a}$$

can be produced by typing

```
The roots of a quadratic polynomial \(a
x^2 + bx + c\) with \(a \neq 0\) are
given by the formula

\[ \frac{-b \pm \sqrt{b^2 - 4ac}}{2a} \]
```

Surds of order n, where n is greater than two, are produced using the control sequence `\sqrt[n]{`*expression*`}`. For example:

> The roots of a cubic polynomial of the form $x^3 - 3px - 2q$ are given by the formula
>
> $$\sqrt[3]{q + \sqrt{q^2 - p^3}} + \sqrt[3]{q - \sqrt{q^2 - p^3}}$$
>
> where the values of the two cube roots must are chosen so as to ensure that their product is equal to p.

can be produced with the input

```
The roots of a cubic polynomial of the
form \(x^3 - 3px - 2q\) are given by
the formula

\[ \sqrt[3]{q + \sqrt{ q^2 - p^3 }}
  + \sqrt[3]{q - \sqrt{ q^2 - p^3 }} \]

where the values of the two cube roots
must are chosen so as to ensure that
their product is equal to \(p\).
```

5.10 Ellipsis (i.e., 'three dots')

The ellipsis symbol is produced in mathematics mode using the control sequences `\ldots` (for dots aligned with tbe base-line of text), and `\cdots` (for dots aligned with the centreline of mathematical formulæ). Thus the formula

$$f(x_1, x_2, \ldots, x_n) = x_1^2 + x_2^2 + \cdots + x_n^2$$

is produced with the input

```
\[ f(x_1, x_2,\ldots, x_n) = x_1^2
        + x_2^2 + \cdots + x_n^2 \]
```

Similarly, the formula

$$\frac{1 - x^{n+1}}{1 - x} = 1 + x + x^2 + \cdots + x^n$$

is produced using `\cdots`, using the input

```
\[ \frac{1 - x^{n+1}}{1 - x} = 1 + x
               + x^2 + \cdots + x^n \]
```

5.11 'Accents' in Maths Mode

There are various control sequences for producing underlining, overlining and various so-called accents in mathematics mode. The following table lists these control sequences, applying them to the letter a:

$\underline{a}$	`\underline{a}`
$\overline{a}$	`\overline{a}`
$\hat{a}$	`\hat{a}`
$\check{a}$	`\check{a}`
$\tilde{a}$	`\tilde{a}`
$\acute{a}$	`\acute{a}`
$\grave{a}$	`\grave{a}`
$\dot{a}$	`\dot{a}`
$\ddot{a}$	`\ddot{a}`
$\breve{a}$	`\breve{a}`
$\bar{a}$	`\bar{a}`
$\vec{a}$	`\vec{a}`

It should be borne in mind that when a character is underlined in a mathematical manuscript then it is normally typeset in bold face without any underlining. Underlining is used very rarely in print.

Control sequences such as `\'` and `\"` used to produce accents in ordinary text may not be used in mathematics mode.

5.12 Brackets and Norms

The frequently used left delimiters include (, [and {, which are obtained by typing `(`, `[` and `\{` respectively. The corresponding right delimiters are of course obtained by typing `)`, `]` and `\}`. In addition, the absolute value, or norm, symbols $|$ and $\|$ are used as both left and right delimiters, and are obtained by typing `|` and `\|` respectively. For example,

> Let X be a Banach space and let $f \colon B \to \textbf{R}$ be a bounded linear functional on X. The *norm* of f, denoted by $\|f\|$, is defined by
>
> $$\|f\| = \inf\{K \in [0, +\infty) : |f(x)| \leq K\|x\| \text{ for all } x \in X\}.$$

is produced by means of the input

```
Let \(X\) be a Banach space and let
\(f \colon B \to \textbf{R}\) be a
bounded linear functional on \(X\). The
```

```
\textit{norm} of \(f\), denoted by
\(\|f\|\), is defined by

\[ \|f\| = \inf \{ K \in [0,+\infty)
           : |f(x)| \leq K \|x\|
           \mbox{ for all } x \in X \}.\]
```

Larger delimiters are sometimes required which have the appropriate height to match the size of the subformula which they enclose. Consider, for instance, the problem of typesetting the formula

$$f(x,y,z) = 3y^2 z \left(3 + \frac{7x+5}{1 + y^2} \right).$$

The way to type the large parentheses is to type `\left(` for the left parenthesis and `\right)` for the right parenthesis, and let LaTeX do the rest of the work. Thus the above formula was obtained by typing

```
\[ f(x,y,z) = 3y^2 z \left( 3
+ \frac{7x+5}{1 + y^2} \right).\]
```

Upon encountering a delimiter preceded by `\left`, LaTeX will search for a corresponding delimiter preceded by `\right` and calculate the size of the delimiters required to enclose the intervening subformula. There is no reason why the enclosing delimiters have to have the same shape; balancing a `\left(` with a `\right]`, for example, is perfectly valid LaTeX syntax, as is nesting pairs of delimiters within one another:

```
\[ \left| 4 x^3 + \left( x
+ \frac{42}{1+x^4} \right)
\right|.\]
```

produces

$$\left| 4x^3 + \left(x + \frac{42}{1+x^4} \right) \right|.$$

The control sequences `\left.` and `\right.` produce *null delimiters* which are completely invisible. Consider, for example, the problem of typesetting

$$\left. \frac{du}{dx} \right|_{x=0}.$$

The vertical bar needs to be big enough to match the fluxion preceding it. Doing this involves telling LaTeX to pretend that the fluxion is enclosed by delimiters, where the left delimiter is invisible and the right delimiter is the vertical line. The invisible delimiter is produced using `\left.` and thus the whole formula is produced by typing

```
\[ \left. \frac{du}{dx} \right|_{x=0}.\]
```

5.13 Multi-Line Formulæ

In didactic literature, it is often necessary to demonstrate the workings of a particular equation. LaTeX provides a method of doing this in the so-called `eqnarray` environment. The following formula is an example of its use:

$$\begin{aligned}\cos 2\theta &= \cos^2\theta - \sin^2\theta \\ &= 2\cos^2\theta - 1.\end{aligned}$$

It is necessary to ensure that the = signs are aligned with one another. The above example was obtained by typing the lines

```
\begin{eqnarray*}
\cos 2\theta & = & \cos^2 \theta
                   - \sin^2 \theta \\
```

```
                & = & 2 \cos^2 \theta - 1.
\end{eqnarray*}
```

Note the use of the special character & as an *alignment tab*. When the formula is typeset, the part of the second line of the formula beginning with an occurrence of & will be placed immediately beneath that part of the first line of the formula which begins with the corresponding occurrence of &. Also, the control sequence \\ is used to separate the lines of the formula.

Although corresponding occurrences of & were placed beneath one another in the above example, it is not necessary (that is, for LaTeX to understand) to do this in the input file. It was done in the above example to improve appearance and to enhance comprehension by *humans*. The more complex example

If $h \leq \frac{1}{2}|\zeta - z|$ then

$$|\zeta - z - h| \geq \frac{1}{2}|\zeta - z|$$

and hence

$$\begin{eqnarray*}
\left| \frac{1}{\zeta - z - h} - \frac{1}{\zeta - z} \right| & = & \left| \frac{(\zeta - z) - (\zeta - z - h)}{(\zeta - z - h)(\zeta - z)} \right| \\
& = & \left| \frac{h}{(\zeta - z - h)(\zeta - z)} \right| \\
& \leq & \frac{2 |h|}{|\zeta - z|^2}.
\end{eqnarray*}$$

was obtained by typing

```
If \(h \leq \frac{1}{2} |\zeta - z|\)
then
\[ |\zeta - z - h| \geq \frac{1}{2}
|\zeta - z|\]
and hence
\begin{eqnarray*}
\left| \frac{1}{\zeta - z - h} -
\frac{1}{\zeta - z} \right| & = &
\left| \frac{(\zeta - z) - (\zeta
- z - h)}{(\zeta - z - h)(\zeta - z)}
\right| \\  & = & \left| \frac{h}{(\zeta
- z - h)(\zeta - z)} \right| \\ & \leq
& \frac{2 |h|}{|\zeta - z|^2}.
\end{eqnarray*}
```

The asterisk in `eqnarray*` is put there to suppress the automatic equation numbering produced by LaTeX. Numbered multi-line formulæ are produced with the control sequences `\begin{eqnarray}` and `\end{eqnarray}`.

5.14 Matrices and other arrays in LaTeX

Matrices and other arrays are produced in LaTeX using the **array** environment. For example, the passage

> The *characteristic polynomial* $\chi(\lambda)$ of the 3×3 matrix
> $$\left(\begin{array}{ccc} a & b & c \\ d & e & f \\ g & h & i \end{array}\right)$$
> is given by the formula
> $$\chi(\lambda) = \left|\begin{array}{ccc} \lambda - a & -b & -c \\ -d & \lambda - e & -f \\ -g & -h & \lambda - i \end{array}\right|.$$

is produced by typing

```
The \emph{characteristic polynomial}
\(\chi(\lambda)\) of the \(3 \times 3\)%
~matrix

\[ \left( \begin{array}{ccc}
a & b & c \\
d & e & f \\
g & h & i \end{array} \right)\]

is given by the formula

\[ \chi(\lambda) = \left|
\begin{array}{ccc}
\lambda - a & -b & -c \\
-d & \lambda - e & -f \\
-g & -h & \lambda - i
\end{array} \right|.\]
```

First of all, note the use of `\left` and `\right` to produce the large delimiters around the arrays. As previously established, the control sequences `\left(` and `\right)` produce delimiters (in this case, parentheses) that expand automatically. Next, note the use of the alignment tab character & to separate the entries of the matrix and the use of \\ to separate the rows of the matrix, exactly as in the construction of multiline formulæ previously described. Finally, as with other environments, LaTeX is told that the array needs special treatment, by use of the control sequences `\begin{array}` and `\end{array}`.

The only thing left to explain, therefore, is the 'mysterious' `{ccc}` which occurs immediately after `\begin{array}`. Each of the c's in `{ccc}` represents a column of the matrix and indicates that the entries of the column should be *centred*. If the `c` were replaced by `l`, the corresponding column would be typeset with all the entries flush *left*, and `r` would produce a column with all entries flush *right*. Thus

```
\[ \begin{array}{lcr}
\mbox{First number} & x & 8 \\
\mbox{Second number} & y & 15 \\
\mbox{Sum} & x + y & 23 \\
\mbox{Difference} & x - y & -7 \\
\mbox{Product} & xy & 120 \end{array}\]
```

produces

First number	x	8
Second number	y	15
Sum	$x + y$	23
Difference	$x - y$	-7
Product	xy	120

We can use the array environment to produce formulæ such as

$$|x| = \left\{ \begin{array}{ll} x & \mbox{if } x \geq 0; \\ -x & \mbox{if } x < 0. \end{array} \right.$$

Note that both columns of this array are set flush left. Thus, `{ll}` is written immediately after `\begin{array}`. The large curly bracket is produced using `\left\{`, but it requires a corresponding `\right` delimiter to match it. As established earlier, the *null delimiter* `\right.` is therefore used to match it. This delimiter is invisible. Thus, the above formula can be constructed by typing

```
\[ |x| = \left\{ \begin{array}{ll}
          x & \mbox{if \(x \geq 0\)};\\
         -x & \mbox{if \(x < 0\)}.
         \end{array} \right. \]
```

5.15 Fluxions, Fluents, Limits, and Series

The expressions

$$\frac{du}{dt} \text{ and } \frac{d^2u}{dx^2}$$

are obtained in LaTeX by typing

```
\frac{du}{dt}
```

and

```
\frac{d^2 u}{dx^2}
```

respectively. The mathematical symbol ∂ is produced using `\partial`. Thus the Heat Equation

$$\frac{\partial u}{\partial t} = \frac{\partial^2 u}{\partial x^2} + \frac{\partial^2 u}{\partial y^2} + \frac{\partial^2 u}{\partial z^2}$$

is obtained in LaTeX by typing

```
\[\frac{\partial u}{\partial t}
   = \frac{\partial^2 u}{\partial x^2}
```

```
        + \frac{\partial^2 u}{\partial y^2}
        + \frac{\partial^2 u}{\partial z^2}
\]
```

Mathematical expressions such as

$$\lim_{x \to +\infty}, \inf_{x > s} \text{ and } \sup_K$$

in displayed equations are produced with the commands `\lim_{x \to +\infty}`, `\inf_{x > s}` and `\sup_K` respectively. Thus, the expression

$$\lim_{x \to +\infty} \frac{3x^2 + 7}{x^2 + 1} = 3.$$

is produced by typing

```
\[ \lim_{x \to +\infty}
\frac{3x^2 +7x^3}{x^2 +5x^4} = 3.\]
```

Arithmetical series, such as

$$\sum_{i=1}^{2n}$$

are entered into LaTeX with a control sequence in the form `sum_{i=1}^{2n}`. Thus

$$\sum_{k=1}^{n} k^2 = \frac{1}{2} n(n+1).$$

is obtained by typing

```
\[ \sum_{k=1}^n k^2 =
\frac{1}{2} n (n+1).\]
```

Geometrical series can be obtained the same way, but `\sum` must be replaced with `\prod`.

It is also possible to obtain *fluents* in mathematical documents. The expression

$$\int_a^b f(x)\,dx.$$

is a typical fluent and is typeset with the LaTeX commands

```
\[ \int_a^b f(x)\,dx.\]
```

The fluent sign $\int$ is typeset using the control sequence `\int`, and the *limits of integration* (in this case a and b are treated as a subscript and a superscript on the fluent sign.

Most fluents occurring in mathematical documents begin with a fluent sign and contain one or more instances of d followed by another (Latin or Greek) letter, as in dx, dy and dt. To obtain the correct appearance, an extra space can be inserted before the d, using \,. Thus

$$\int_0^{+\infty} x^n e^{-x} \,dx = n!.$$

$$\int \cos\theta \,d\theta = \sin\theta.$$

$$\int_{x^2+y^2\leq R^2} f(x,y)\,dx\,dy = \int_{\theta=0}^{2\pi} \int_{r=0}^{R} f(r\cos\theta, r\sin\theta) r\,dr\,d\theta.$$

and

$$\int_0^R \frac{2x\,dx}{1+x^2} = \log(1+R^2).$$

are obtained by typing
j

```
\[ \int_0^{+\infty} x^n e^{-x} \,dx = n!.\]

\[ \int \cos \theta \,d\theta
= \sin \theta.\]
```

```
\[ \int_{x^2 + y^2 \leq R^2} f(x,y)\,dx\,dy
 = \int_{\theta=0}^{2\pi}
   \int_{r=0}^R f(r\cos\theta, r\sin\theta)
   r\,dr\,d\theta.\]
```

and

```
\[ \int_0^R \frac{2x\,dx}{1+x^2} =
   \log(1+R^2).\]
```

respectively.

In some multiple fluents (i.e., those containing more than one fluent sign) one finds that LaTeX puts too much space between the signs. The way to improve the appearance of the fluent is to use the control sequence `\!` to remove a thin strip of unwanted space (that is, to add a thin *negative* space). Thus, for example, the double fluent

$$\int_0^1 \! \int_0^1 x^2 y^2 \, dx \, dy.$$

is obtained by typing

```
\[ \int_0^1 \! \int_0^1 x^2
   y^2\,dx\,dy.\]
```

Had

```
\[ \int_0^1 \int_0^1 x^2
   y^2\,dx\,dy.\]
```

been typed instead,

$$\int_0^1 \int_0^1 x^2 y^2\,dx\,dy.$$

would have been obtained.

A particularly noteworthy example comes when typesetting a multiple fluent such as

$$\int \!\!\! \int_D f(x,y)\,dx\,dy.$$

Here, \! is used three times in succession to obtain suitable spacing between the fluent signs. We typeset this fluent using

```
\[ \int \!\!\! \int_D f(x,y)\,dx\,dy.\]
```

Had

```
\[ \int \int_D f(x,y)\,dx\,dy.\]
```

been typed instead,

$$\int \int_D f(x, y)\, dx\, dy.$$

would have been obtained.

The following (reasonably complex) passage exhibits a number of the features which have been discussed:

> In non-relativistic wave mechanics, the wave function $\psi(\mathbf{r}, t)$ of a particle satisfies the *Schrödinger Wave Equation*
>
> $$i\hbar \frac{\partial\psi}{\partial t} = \frac{-\hbar^2}{2m} \left(\frac{\partial^2}{\partial x^2} + \frac{\partial^2}{\partial y^2} + \frac{\partial^2}{\partial z^2} \right) \psi + V\psi.$$
>
> It is customary to normalize the wave equation by demanding that
>
> $$|\psi(\mathbf{r}, t)|^2\, dx\, dy\, dz = 0,$$
>
> and hence
>
> $$\iiint_{\mathbf{R}^3} |\psi(\mathbf{r}, t)|^2\, dx\, dy\, dz = 1$$

for all times t. If we normalize the wave function in this way then, for any (measurable) subset V of $\mathbf{R}^3$ and time t,

$$\iiint_V |\psi(\mathbf{r},t)|^2 \, dx \, dy \, dz$$

represents the probability that the particle is to be found within the region V at time t.

One would typeset this as follows:

```
\In non-relativistic wave mechanics,
the wave function \(\psi(\mathbf{r},t)\)
of a particle satisfies the \textit{%
Schr\"{o}dinger Wave Equation}
\[ i\hbar\frac{\partial \psi}{\partial t}
  = \frac{-\hbar^2}{2m} \left(
    \frac{\partial^2}{\partial x^2}
    + \frac{\partial^2}{\partial y^2}
    + \frac{\partial^2}{\partial z^2}
  \right) \psi + V \psi.\]
It is customary to normalise the wave
equation by demanding that
\[ \int \!\!\! \int \!\!\! \int_{\textbf{R}^3}
```

```
      \left| \psi(\mathbf{r},0)
      \right|^2\,dx\,dy\,dz = 1.\]
A simple calculation using the
Schr\"{o}dinger wave equation shows that
\[ \frac{d}{dt} \int \!\!\!
   \int \!\!\! \int_{\textbf{R}^3}
   \left| \psi(\mathbf{r},t)
   \right|^2\,dx\,dy\,dz = 0,\]
and hence
\[ \int \!\!\! \int \!\!\! \int_{\textbf{R}^3}
  \left| \psi(\mathbf{r},t)
  \right|^2\,dx\,dy\,dz = 1\]
for all times~\(t\). If we normalize
the wave function in this way then, for
any (measurable) subset~\(V\) of
\(\textbf{R}^3\)
and time~\(t\),
\[ \int \!\!\! \int \!\!\! \int_V
   \left| \psi(\mathbf{r},t)
   \right|^2\,dx\,dy\,dz\]
represents the probability that the
particle is to be found within the
region~\(V\) at time~\(t\).
```

www.ingramcontent.com/pod-product-compliance
Ingram Content Group UK Ltd.
Pitfield, Milton Keynes, MK11 3LW, UK
UKHW020130250726
13967UKWH00002B/571